Sadhu Sundar Singh
Called of God

Mrs. Arthur Parker
(Rebecca Jane Parker)
London Missionary Society, Trivandram, S. India

Original published by Fleming H. Revell Co., New York, 1920

Updated Edition
Trumpet Press, Lawton, OK

Author: Parker, Rebeecca Jane
Title: Sadhu Sundar Singh, Called of God
1. evangelism 2. Christian mysticism 3. Christian biography

ISBN: 978-0615938486

Trumpet Press is a member of the Christian Small Publishers Association (CSPA).

Also available from Trumpet Press:

The Message of Sadhu Sundar Singh: A Study in Mysticism on Practical Religion, by Burnett Hillman Streeter, and A. J. Appasamy

The Visions of Sadhu Sundar Singh, by Sadhu Sundar Singh.

Table of Contents

Also available from Trumpet Press:

The Message of Sadhu Sundar Singh: A Study in Mysticism on Practical Religion, by Burnett Hillman Streeter, and A. J. Appasamy

The Visions of Sadhu Sundar Singh, by Sadhu Sundar Singh.

Sadhu Sundar Singh

Note From the Publisher

This biography was originally published in 1920, but this edition contains the further journeys of Sundar through 1922 added to the 4th American edition. He spent 1925-1927 quietly writing, then in 1929 he made another trip to Tibet and was never seen or heard from again (1889-1929).

Mrs. Parker was British, so it originally had British spelling of some words which were changed to U.S. spelling. Some words were updated, some were not, and some words that will be unknown to most readers were defined in brackets [..].

The foreign words and place-names were left untouched, but most were checked to be sure they were spelled correctly.

And the Roman numerals were changed to modern numbers.

Foreword and Letter

This little book was originally intended for the use of Christian women of the Malayalam country, but the writer has been persuaded to issue an English edition.

Nearly the whole of the matter has been the subject of conversations with Sadhu himself, with whom we have enjoyed much inspiring companionship and with whose permission the book is issued.

This word picture of a true servant of the Great Master should be an inspiration to all Christian men and women in India, and it does not seem too much to hope that Indians of all classes will see how truly Jesus Christ can manifest Himself in and through the people of this great land, and how worthy He is to be India's Lord and Savior.

Arthur Parker
London Mission, Trivandram
***

A Letter From Sadhu Sundar Singh
(Written in Roman-Urdu)

Jab main is ehhothi kitab ka MSS dekh raha tha to yih bat safai so dekhne men ai ki Khuda ki Ruh ne kaise ajib taur se Mrs. R. J. Parker ki madad aur hidayat ki, ki sari baten bagair kisi galati ki likhin, aur mujhe yaqin hai, ki musannif ki mihnat Khuda ke jalal aur bahuton ke ruhani faida ki bais hogi. Aur unko mada milegi jo mushkilat men hain, jis tarah ki main tha, aur khass kar yih malum, karke, ki Khudawand kis tarah mujhe jaise bare gunahgar ko bacha kar apni muhabbat aur fazl se apni khidmat ke liye chun leta hai. Aj main shukarguzari ke sath apne tajruba 18 baras ke experience se kah sakta hun ki Masih aj kal aur hamesha yaksan hai (Hebrews 13:8).

Meri dua hai ki Khuda in chand baton ke auron ki ruhani madad aur apni jalal ke liye istianal kare. Amin.

(Signed) Sundar Singh

September 8, 1918

Translation

When I saw the manuscript of this little book I saw clearly in what a wonderful way the spirit of God had helped and guided Mrs. R. J. Parker so that she had written it without any mistake, and I am certain that the author's work will be for the glory of God and a means of spiritual benefit to many. Also that those who are in the midst of difficulties such as I was, will receive help, and especially will learn how the Lord saved so great a sinner as myself, and by His love and grace chose me for His service.

Today I can say with thankfulness after thirteen years of experience that Christ is the same yesterday, and today, and forever (Hebrews 13:8).

My prayer is that God will use these few words for His glory and for the spiritual help of others. Amen.

(Signed) Sundar Singh

September 8, 1918

Hast thou heard Him, seen Him, known Him,
Is not thine a captured heart?
Chief among ten thousand own Him,
Joyful choose the better part.

What has stripped the seeming beauty
From the idols of the earth?
Not a sense of right or duty,
But the sight of peerless worth.

Not the crushing of those idols,
With its bitter void and smart;
But the beaming of His beauty,
The unveiling of His heart!

'Tis that look that melted Peter,
'Tis that face that Stephen saw,
'Tis that heart that wept with Mary
Can alone from idols draw.

Draw and win and fill completely,
Till the cup o'erflow the brim;
What have we to do with idols
Who have companied with Him?

****

To
My Dear Husband
who through thirty years
has kept me faithful
to the best things
of life.

Introduction

February, 1918, is a time that will linger in the memory of Christians of all denominations in Trivandram, for the visit of Sadhu Sundar Singh was an unprecedented event that brought to many profound spiritual blessing. One of our missionaries rightly said, "Such a figure has never passed through the Indian Church before"; and in passing he left the deep consciousness that God had visited His people.

The fame of the Sadhu had preceded him, for a few had read the books published about his life and work, and of these some looked for a day of miracles to dawn. Most, however, were filled with desire to see and hear him that they might receive the spiritual blessings they believed possible from his ministry. That God did not disappoint these hopes there are numbers today who could give joyful testimony.

As the train bringing Sadhu Sundar Singh to Trivandram drew into the station, besides the missionary, a group of Indian Christians stood ready to accord a welcome to him; and upon arrival at the Mission House a crowd had gathered for the same purpose, and would hardly be persuaded to disperse in order to allow the Sadhu to get a wash and some food.

A Wesleyan missionary thus describes the appearance of the Sadhu: "The Sadhu has a noble presence. He is tall, with a well-shaped head and fine features. . . . His hands and feet are delicately formed and exquisitely kept. He is scrupulously clean in person and attire. The only dress he wears is the long orange robe of the ascetic, which falls in graceful and dignified folds about his body. No one can look upon him for the first time without being struck by his close likeness to the traditional portrait of Christ."

There are many things in this old land that give a fresh understanding of the Bible, but no man of my experience has made us realize so fully how our Savior lived and moved about in His day. During his visit to Trivandram, whenever Sadhu Sundar Singh appeared in public, wondering crowds followed him. Even the children gathered behind him that they might touch his yellow robe, and the sick were brought that he might pray with them. It is almost impossible to convince the people that he does not heal the sick, even when the assurance comes from his own lips.

At one of his meetings a pathetic incident occurred that brought vividly to mind how our Lord was sought. It was at a large open-air meeting. Some men appeared carrying a sick man on a bed. They placed it gently upon the ground in a place where the afflicted man could behold the face and hear the words of the Sadhu. He was a Christian from a village seven miles away, and had been brought in overnight so as to be present at this great gathering.

That very night another incident took place that reminded us of the visit of Nicodemus to our Savior. At two o'clock, when all the world was locked in sleep, a low rapping at the door announced the arrival of a midnight guest. A caste man desirous of discussing religious matters had come to see him. When explaining that he had felt ashamed to come in the daylight the Sadhu replied, "Jesus Christ was not ashamed to suffer for you on the cross in the daylight, so cannot you suffer a little for Him?" At the service next day this gentleman took his courage in both hands, and appeared amongst the crowd of Christians to listen to the Sadhu preaching.

Sundar Singh has brought fresh visions of God and Christ to us all, and many of us realize how by close fellowship with Jesus, and complete obedience to His will, he has become so conformed to his Lord that wherever he goes people say, "How like Christ he is!"

To see and hear him makes one's heart beat high with hope for India's future, and with confidence that the day will come when the east will have some new aspect of our Savior to discover to the west. For thirty years we have waited for men to rise up who can reach the heart of India, and surely none has come nearer to doing this than this humble lover of the Cross", Sadhu Sundar Singh.

Chapter 1
Sadhu and Sanyasi

Perhaps in no country in the world is more importance attached to the proper observances of religion than in India, and the greatest reverence is felt towards men who adopt a religious life. For ages Indians have learnt to place the man who renounces the world above him who rules and conquers it. The power of the priest is too well known to need mention here, and although the spread of western education has done much to undermine his influence, the family priest still reigns supreme in the homes of India. But outside the priestly caste there are numbers of men who take up a religious life, and chief amongst them are those known as sadhus and sanyasis. There is often confusion between these terms, and they are supposed to be identical. The main difference seems to be that the sadhu's is a life vowed to religion from the beginning, while the sanyasi's may begin at any time, even in old age.

Many Indians desire to consecrate their last years to religion, so they cast off all family ties and all worldly ambitions and responsibilities, and for the remainder of their days practice the austerities of the sanyasi life. It is generally understood that such men have fulfilled all the ordinary obligations of life, having married and had a family, and done a share of the world's work.

A sadhu, however, early in life renounces the world and all its pleasures. He never marries or enters upon the ordinary occupations of the world.

The sadhu life is one of untold possibilities, of tremendous temptations: a life that commands the respectful attention of India, for it is a type of heroism which dares to lose the world and all the world may offer in its absolute self-abandonment. To one who perfectly carries out this ideal, the proudest head in India will always bow in reverence and humility. Both sanyasi and sadhu adopt the saffron robe-the time honored dress which gives them the freedom of all India. The simplicity of their life is such that they have no home and carry no money, and amongst Hindus it is an act of religious merit to provide them with shelter and food.

From the earliest days this kind of life has had great attractions for the pious minds of India, and during the centuries men have voluntarily sacrificed the world and all it stands for, that by all kinds of hardships and self-denial they might satisfy the deep longings of the soul. Numberless times men of noble aspiration have by this means striven to obtain peace of soul and absorption in the deity.

The commonest sight in any of the holy cities of India is that of one or many sadhus practicing the austerities of their chosen lot, either by swinging over a slow fire, holding up the right arm until it has stiffened and the nails have grown through the back of the hand, sitting on a bed of spikes, or under a vow of silence in meditation on the banks of some sacred stream. Unfortunately this kind of life has been subject to the most terrible abuse, and there is scarcely a more disgusting sight in the world than the filthy beggar who, donning the saffron robe, passes from house to house terrorizing the ignorant inhabitants, and cursing them when he cannot wring from their unwilling hands the gifts he asks.

The ordinary winter visitor to India cannot but be impressed by the numerous signs he sees in all the holy places he passes through, that many Indians are seeking God, "if haply they might feel after Him and find Him." And while the sight of numberless filthy fakirs awakens a sense of disgust and repulsion, surely no Christian man can see the self-torture of many sanyasis without a deep yearning to discover to them the great secret of the peace they so arduously strive to find.

In India life can be lived at its simplest. The climate enables men to do with little clothing, and to live largely an out-of-door life. Except where the stream of western life has turned men aside to greater luxury, the Indian still feels satisfied with a simple diet and life. Hence through the centuries, as earnest souls have gone in quest of higher spiritual things, it is not surprising that they have chosen the simplest possible life, and added to its hardships by self-imposed austerities.

To people of western nations, with their harder climate and different customs, such simplicity is impossible, and to many even difficult to understand. The true sadhu does not retire to a monastery where food and shelter are assured. He wanders homeless from place to place, possesses only the meagre clothes he wears, and is utterly destitute.

Dr. Farquhar, in his Crown of Hinduism, says :-

As long as the world lasts men will look back with wonder on the ascetics of India. Their quiet surrender of every earthly privilege, and their strong endurance of many forms of suffering will be an inspiration to all generations of thinking Indians. For nearly three thousand years the ascetics of India have stood forth, a speaking testimony to the supremacy of the spiritual.

The ideal is a great one. Christianize this ideal, make it a renunciation for the sake of others, that remaining "in the world but not of it" a man "shall endure all things" in an untiring search for other souls, and we have the noblest life attainable on earth.

Chapter 2
Sundar Singh As Sadhu

The Christian Patriot, a Madras paper, recently published the following:-

Sadhu Sundar Singh is the embodiment of an idea running in the veins of every Indian, and inherited by him from the distant past. Standing before men as the homeless Sadhu, not knowing where his next meal will come from, without worldly goods, he recalls to men's minds in these days the great ideal of renunciation.

But in this case the ideal is realized in perfection, since not for his own soul, but for the souls of others, he "counts all things but loss"; and his great renunciation, entailing untold hardship, privation, suffering, and persecution, is his daily offering to the Savior who gave His life for him.

Obeying the wishes of his dead and greatly loved mother, Sundar unflinchingly faced the anger of. his Hindu relatives, the ridicule of his Christian brethren, and even the mild hostility of his European friends, and became a Christian Sadhu. Thirty-three days after his baptism, when only a boy of sixteen, he took this step in the firm belief that God had called him to this particular kind of life and work. Since that day he has never ceased to interpret the life of Him who had not where to lay His head to Indians who have been taught to revere a holy life of self-denial. Thus does he commend to his countrymen in truly eastern manner the great things for which the Savior gave His life. This new method of preaching Christ has laid the Sadhu open to a considerable amount of criticism in the past, but in the form of a parable he explains that a Hindu will not drink water from a foreign vessel even when dying of thirst, but if that same water be offered to him in his own brass vessel he will accept it.

It may be that the time has come when Indian Christians must venture upon new forms of spiritual enterprise, for they know the needs of their own countrymen, have received the same traditions, and have the same outlook on life. Beyond question the Sadhu's new venture has brought untold blessing to many thousands all over this great land of India.

By adopting the recognized dress of the sadhu, Sundar Singh not only opens the door to all castes and classes of society, but also even to the sacred precincts of the Banana homes of India, where on various occasions he has had unique opportunities of speaking for his Lord to the great ladies of the land. His own words are:-

The day I became a Sadhu I was wedded to these garments, and I will never divorce them of my own will.

He has frequently been asked how long he means to continue this life of self-abnegation, to which he replies:

As long as I am in this world, I have vowed my life to Him, and His. grace abiding I shall never break my vow.

Never long in one place, he wanders over the length and breadth of India, meeting with all sorts and conditions of men, suffering the changes of climate from the steamy tropical heat of Travancore and Ceylon to the icy cold of Tibet. Without knowledge of how food or raiment or lodging shall be provided from day to day, carrying no money or worldly possessions, Sadhu Sundar Singh continues his pilgrimage in the service of his fellow-men and to the glory of his Master Christ. In cold or heat he wears the same clothes, and even in the bitter cold of farthest Tibet he wears no shoes, for by "his bleeding feet he attracts men to Christ." Wherever he goes he carries a small copy of the New Testament in Urdu, which with the help of nature and his own experience is all he needs to enforce his powerful teaching.

In his book, *The Manhood of the Master,* Dr. Fosdick says that "Jesus must have been the most radiant Man of His time in Palestine." Looking at Sadhu Sundar Singh it is easy to realize this, for to him suffering for Christ is a real joy, and his face is expressive of the deep peace and abounding joy he has in his dearest Savior, Christ. During fourteen years of sadhu life Sundar Singh has known all manner of trials, and endured much suffering and persecution. Like his great predecessor Paul, he has been "troubled on every side . . . perplexed, but not in despair; persecuted but not forsaken; cast down but not destroyed; always bearing about in the body the dying of the Lord Jesus, that the life also of Jesus may be made manifest" in his body (2 Cor. 4:7-10).

Chapter 3
Sundar The Man

A Western missionary who has loved India through a long life may perhaps be pardoned for writing this chapter. Ever since meeting Sundar Singh the question as to the great difference between him and most other Christians, and also the Sadhu's unusual power of drawing men to Christ, has been uppermost in his mind. Absolute loss of all things and an entire submission to the will of Christ together with a profound enthralling love for his Savior gives at least a partial answer to the problem.

In India as in our Lord's day "to the poor the Gospel is preached," and has found acceptance, and brought to many thousands a better life and a freer heritage. In some cases there is trouble and loss and even persecution, but the cases are few and far between where absolute loss of all things is the price of following Christ.

But, as will be seen in a succeeding chapter, the conversion of Sundar to Christ brought with it not only the loss of all things but great persecution and hardship. All he got by becoming a Christian was Christ; and this incomparable gift swamped everything else, so that since that time it has been an ecstasy of delight to him to suffer with and for his Master. When more of India's sons accept the Savior in this spirit, the Christian Church in this land will enter into her rightful heritage and become the evangelizing power that shall bring India to her Savior.

Wherein lies Sundar Singh's power to draw men to Christ? Early in life he had an awakened conscience, and for long sought peace in the sacred books with which he was familiar. Failing to find in them what he sought he turned to the New Testament. Imagine his ardent and highly-strung mind intent on the story of Christ as related there! A new Book-not a worn-out creed, nor the story of how Old Testament prophecies had been fulfilled, nor yet a thing he had read from a child and grown accustomed to! There was no staleness in the Gospel story to him. Christ walked this earth again, lived and spoke in every line; and as he read, the marvel of the story grew, until obsessed by the vision he counted all things as dross that he "might win Christ and be found in Him." He had no books to explain the New Testament or to cloud its meaning. There were just the New Testament, God and his own highly attuned soul-a soul that had sought long and hopelessly for God, and had found here all, and more than he had sought.

The picture of this Hindu boy sitting under a tree out of sight of friend, or foe, immersed in the reading of his Urdu Testament and sobbing over its contents, is one that brings tears to the eyes, and calls us to pause and ask ourselves, "Have we so learned Christ?" It takes us back to foundation things, and stripped of our learning and knowledge we cry out for that same simple experience-just to meet Christ as he did.

From those days to the present, Sundar Singh has wandered in company with his Lord over the length and breadth of India, with his Urdu New Testament in his hand, and with Christ in his heart, and a look of Christ upon his face.

In The Goal of India the Rev. W. E. S. Holland says:

> India is the spiritual mother of half mankind. . . . No book that sets out to unveil for other peoples the heart of India could put anything else but religion in the very forefront. ... To the Indian that is all that really matters . . . nothing else can ever satisfy his soul. The climax of India's religious ideal has ever been renunciation. There is something of the magnificent in the sadhu's measureless contempt for suffering and hardship. . . . Christ will redeem India's ancient ideal: India needs to see Christ as well as hear about Him. . . . India needs the simple Christian, who in a life of gentleness and patience, of lowly love and humble service, will unveil to her the beauty of Christ.

Herein lies one great secret of Sadhu Sundar Singh's power over men wherever he goes. Taking the old ideal' of renunciation he has spiritualized it, and men see in him a reflection of the great renunciation of Christ Himself-not seeking suffering for suffering's own sake, as is the case with Hindu asceticism, but enduring it with cheerful acceptance as being the will of God for him. In the words of Keshab Chandra Sen :-

Behold Christ cometh to us as an Asiatic ... to fulfill and perfect that religion of communion for which India has been panting-yea, after long centuries shall this communion be perfected in Christ.

Sadhu Sundar Singh in himself reminds men of this great fact, and looking beyond him they "Behold the Man" who "for our sakes became poor."

Can one wonder that whenever he makes his public appearances large crowds gather to hear him? India must be won for Christ by her own sons, and in Sundar Singh we see a man whose appeal goes straight to the heart of an Indian, be he Christian or otherwise. His appearance, his utter self-abnegation and poverty, his presentation of the Gospel message, even the manner of his conversion combine to make that appeal irresistible to the people of India. They understand and believe in such a man. Thus this son of India possesses a key to the hearts of his countrymen no foreigner can ever hope to have, however great his love for India and her people may be.

An Indian gentleman thus speaks of him:-

A tall young man in flowing toga and a short black beard delivering his message with the fire of a prophet and the power of an apostle 1 As the sweet words flowed from his lips the Sadhu stood before us as a symbol of the spiritual culture of the East set aglow in the resplendent light of the Gospel.

While an American adds:-

The beauty that he daily gazes upon draws the deep souls of India who have not yet beheld it, but have seen it in him. His life is his power, and that life has to be lived to make that power felt.

The Young Men of India for July, 1918, publishes the following:-

It is almost an impossible task to present any appreciation of him (the Sadhu) in words. He is a man who has taken up the life of a sadhu because he believes that God has called him to this method of labor for Him. He utterly disowns the idea that in the life of the sadhu there is any intrinsic and special holiness. . . , His addresses, like his personality, are radiant with a calm, deep and glowing faith in God, and it is impossible to be in his company without realizing that he is one to whom God is a familiar friend. . . . He conveys the message which is the heart of his own life through addresses filled with vivid and often piquant illustrations drawn from his own experience . . . and he presses home his points with unforgettable similes and illustrations. It is a fortunate thing for the Indian Church that the first man who has become widely known as a Christian Sadhu should be one of such simple humble faith, and so purely a Christian personality.

The Sadhu is not emotional or fanatical. Every gift he possesses he ascribes to Christ, and to Christ alone. He belongs to no sect and is not a member of any order. In himself he calls Indians back to simplicity, self-sacrifice, and a pure whole-hearted devotion to Christ, that seeks only after God and works perpetually for the souls of men. Life to him is only of value so far as it serves these great ends, and standing before men as the embodiment of these ideals his appeal to India is irresistible.

Chapter 4
Nationality and Birth

Sadhu Sundar Singh is a Sikh by birth. The Sikhs are, for various reasons, of peculiar interest. Arising first as a religious sect resolved to reform abuses and to lead men back to a simpler purer worship, they eventually developed into an organized military power. Through four centuries they have had many and hitter experiences, but pride of race, love of arms, and a stiff clinging to their religious doctrines, are to this day their great characteristics.

Cunningham, in his History of the Sikhs, says:-

> During the sixteenth century while the Punjab was a scene of endless contention for power amongst foreign races, the religious sect of the Sikhs, humble in its origin, unpretending in its primitive character, silently arose amidst the tumult of arms, and in spite of persecution laid the foundations of a great state.

The home of the Sikhs is "The Country of the Five Rivers," and a remarkable circumstance of the population of the Punjab is the comparative paucity of the Sikhs in a country once ruled by them. The Sikhs do not form a numerous sect, yet their strength is not to be estimated by numbers, but by their unity and energy of religious fervor and warlike temperament. They will dare and endure much; they arc not easily discouraged by defeat; and they look forward hopefully to the day when the double mission of Nanak and Govind Singh shall become a dominant religion.

Some further account of the Sikhs will be found at the end of the book, and from it will be seen some of the national and religious influences under which Sundar Singh was born. Captain Cunningham says:-

> A Sikh chief is not more distinguished by his stately person and manly bearing than a minister of his faith is by a lofty thoughtfulness of look, which marks the fervor of his soul, and his persuasion of the near presence of the Divinity. In religious faith and worldly aspiration they are wholly different from other Indians.

From such a stock sprang Sundar Singh. His father was Sirdar Sher Singh, a Sikh by descent, and to this day a wealthy landowner in Rampur, in the State of Patiala, where on September 8, 1889, Sundar was born; the youngest son in the family, but called to a higher destiny than them all. One of the family is Sirdar A. Nath Singh, commander of an Indian force in one of the Sikh States, while others have risen to even higher distinction still.

As a child Sundar was brought up in the lap of luxury. Every year as the hot weather drew on, he was taken with the family to spend the summer in the cooler air of the Himalayas, usually to Simla.

His mother was a refined and gifted lady; very broadminded in her sympathies. She was on friendly terms with the American Presbyterian Mission ladies, and permitted their visits to her home. From his earliest days the relationship between Sundar and his mother was of the tenderest character. He was the youngest of the family, and he seldom left her side. She would often say to him, "You must not be careless and worldly like your brothers. You must seek peace of soul and love religion, and some day you must become a holy sadhu."

So frequently did he hear such words as these from his mother's lips that he never contemplated any other life than this of which she spoke. Wherever she went her little son accompanied her, and she never ceased to teach him the best things she knew. By the time he was seven years of age he had learnt the Bhagavad-Gita from beginning to end in Sanskrit. And then, at the age of fourteen, Sundar lost his dearest earthly friend. How he missed her gentle companionship no one knows, but today when he speaks of her his voice grows tender, and he believes that were she alive she would be satisfied to see him living and working as he is this day.

Chapter 5
Called To Seek

"Ye shall seek Me and find Me when ye shall search for Me with all your heart."-Jeremiah 29:18.

It has often been remarked that great men owe much to the early training given by their mothers, and in the case of Sadhu Sundar Singh this is especially true. From his earliest days the child not only accompanied his mother on her visits to the temples but was carefully taught by her to regard religion as the supreme thing in life. He saw her reverence for the holy men she often went to consult, and very early in life his impressionable mind seized upon the idea that of all lives that of a holy sadhu was the best worth living.

Sundar learnt from his devout mother that there was a peace of heart which needed earnest seeking, and which, when found, would be the greatest treasure on earth. So frequently did she speak of this to him that as he grew in understanding the desire to gain this precious gift grew in intensity. The little child who had "rubbed his forehead on the temple door" and sat at the feet of Hindu holy men, now began to seek for the inestimable treasure he had learnt to regard as the one thing worth obtaining in the world.

The Granth of the Sikhs, the sacred books of the Hindu religion, and even the Qur'an of the Muhammadans, were all ceaselessly read and searched. Often when his family lay asleep Sundar would sit poring over the pages of one or other of these books. Many passages and verses he learnt by heart, and yet with all his increasing knowledge there only came to him a deeper unrest of soul.

The priests of the temple, the sadhus he so often saw, and even his pious mother, failed to bring him rest of heart, although they quoted many passages from their sacred books in the hope of helping him. Thus built up in, but unsatisfied with, the faith of his fathers, and without knowledge of Christ and Christianity, Sundar was sent to learn at the mission school carried on by the American Presbyterians in his own village. Here every day the Bible was taught, and Sundar heard things that aroused in his mind feelings of the deepest antagonism.

His Sikh blood was roused on the very first day by his being told to read the Bible. "Why should I? We are Sikhs and the Granth is our sacred book." But Sundar, with a friend of his own age and standing, were persuaded to obey the rule of the school, and then he bought for himself a copy of the New Testament and began to read it. But his horror was only increased when he found its teaching utterly subversive of all he had learnt and treasured from his childhood. A deep inbred reverence for his own religion, almost amounting to fanaticism, roused him beyond endurance. Soon he became the ringleader of the boys in the school who hated Christianity. Openly he tore up the hated pages of his New Testament and burnt them in the fire. Hearing of this his father expostulated with him, declaring the Bible to be a good book, and telling him that he should have returned it to the missionary rather than have treated it thus.

Again Sundar turned to his own sacred books, this time with an abhorrence for Christ and a greater determination to find the peace of which his mother had taught him. He not only arduously studied the Indian religious systems and holy books, but also practiced "Yoga" under a Hindu sadhu, and learnt how to throw himself into mystic trances, which brought temporary relief, although when he came out of the trance he was more miserable than before. He was taken away from the mission school and sent to a government school three miles away from his home. The daily long walk in the fierce Indian sun soon began to tell on his health, and before long it became apparent that he must return to the mission school if he was to finish his education.

All this time he had been diligent in his search for peace, and the constant cry of his heart was for shanti -that comprehensive Hindi term that means not only peace but a full satisfaction of soul. But the more he longed the greater was his disappointment when he found himself growingly filled with a deep soul-hunger that nothing would satisfy.

Back in the mission school Sundar once more found the Gospel in his hand, and again listened to the daily teaching of the Bible. Then returned upon him his old hatred of Christianity, and the very name of Christ filled his mind with angry resentment. So strong were his feelings at that time that on one occasion, when the shadow of a Christian missionary fell across him, he spent a whole hour in washing away the pollution. Sundar speaks of this period as one of the most trying of his life, for he had come to the end of his own religion without discovering the shanti he was in search of, and his deep-rooted hatred of Christianity prevented him from even looking into the Christian sacred book for this "pearl of great price."

Chapter 6
Called Of God

"Blessed are they 'that hunger and thirst after righteousness: for they shall be filled."-Matthew 5:6.

"Come unto Me . . . and I will give you rest."-Matthew 11:28.

Thus far God had led Sundar by a way he knew not, and it seemed only to lead him into blacker night. Having studied line by line all the religions he knew, having heard from the lips of many religious teachers all they had to tell, and in spite of all still experiencing a deeper and more unsatisfied longing for the shanti he believed possible, Sundar was led by God to see that in none of these things could he find what he sought. In the silent sanctuary of his own heart came the thought at last, that perhaps in the despised book he had so furiously destroyed there might be some help, and so he yet again took the Testament in hand. Torn with anguish and driven to despair he read there, "Come unto Me . . . and I will give you rest." The words arrested him, and as he continued to read the story of the cross the wonder grew. No longer did he join with His class-mates in their open abuse of the Christian religion. Sometimes he was discovered in quiet converse with the Christian teacher. Eventually these things were noticed and duly reported to his parents, but his father took little notice, for the boy had been well grounded in the Sikh religion by his devout mother, and was imbued with its beliefs.

But the leaven of the Gospel had entered his heart, and as he read, "God so loved the world that He gave His only begotten Son, that whosoever believeth on Him should not perish but have everlasting life," a whisper of comfort came to his sore heart. But still the burden of anguish prevented him finding rest. At last he felt he must put an end to the struggle. So one night he made a firm resolve that he would obtain peace before dawn- either in this world or the next. He knew that at five o'clock each morning the Ludhiana express passed at the bottom of his father's garden, and to end his misery seemed no sin to the Hindu boy.

In Hindu fashion he bathed, and with Testament in hand he retired to his room to spend the long night in reading, meditation and prayer. Just before dawn Sundar became conscious of a bright cloud filling the room, and in the cloud he saw the radiant figure and face of Christ. As he looked upon the vision it seemed to him that Christ spoke saying, "Why do you oppose Me? I am your Savior. I died on the cross for you." His determined enmity was broken down for ever as he looked upon that Face so filled with Divine love and pity, and with conviction came a sublime sense of forgiveness and acceptance with Christ. At that moment there flashed into his heart the great shanti he had sought so long. Rising from his knees the vision faded, but from that hour Christ has remained with him, and shanti has been his dearest possession. With a heart brimming over with joy Sundar went to his father's room and told him that he was a Christian. Unable to believe that his son could be in earnest, the father urged him to go to rest, and believing all was right he fell asleep again. But that memorable night the thorn-crowned Jesus had called Sundar Singh to follow in His steps, and from that night the cross of Jesus was to be his joyous theme, until that cross shall lift him into the presence of his Savior for evermore.

Chapter 7
Called To Suffer-1

"A man's foes shall be they of his own household."-Matt. 10:30.

"For unto you it is given in the behalf of Christ, not only to believe on Him, but also to suffer for His sake."- Phil. 1:29.

For nine months from that night onwards Sundar Singh was to pass from sorrow to sorrow, until he had drunk the cup of suffering to its bitterest dregs, for all that time he remained in his father's house.

When it became known that he had chosen Jesus as his master, it seemed too heinous a thing for any member of his family to believe. That one of their number, belonging as they did to a proud and influential family, should dream of joining the despised sect of the Christians, none could contemplate. The father, with much earnest pleading and tenderness, urged his son to put aside such degrading and foolish thoughts; to remember the high estate he had been born to, and the noble prospects that lay before him. He unrolled before the eyes of Sundar visions of Wealth and honor, of high positions awaiting him; but, seeing these things made no impression, he portrayed to him the shame and disgrace that would befall his family if he persisted in his present course. The father knew his son's heart, and the love that heart still held for his mother and kindred.

None but Sundar can tell the temptations of that dreadful hour. Anguish filled his soul that he should bring reproach on those he loved. At that moment too were spread before him the temptations, ambitions and glitter of the world; and once more he was to feel the power of earth's attractions and earth's love. But God had not called Sundar from despair and darkness to let him fall a prey to these temptations. It seemed to him that Jesus whispered, "He that loveth father or mother more than Me is not worthy of Me, and he that taketh not his cross and followeth Me is not worthy of Me." Only when he saw his father's tears did poor Sundar's heart almost break, but even as he declared his love for his father he had strength given to speak of a greater love for One who had called him to follow Him, and whom he could not disobey. Such scenes of pathos are not to be dwelt upon in the pages of a book.

About this time, when it was fully realized that Sundar had made up his mind to follow Christ, a fresh attempt was made to turn him aside and to win him back to his old faith. An honored uncle, the possessor of great wealth, one day took him off to his large house, and led him to a deep cellar below the main building. Taking him inside the uncle locked the door and Sundar wondered whether his last hour had come. But, taking a key, his uncle stepped forward and unlocked a large safe. Throwing open the door there was revealed to the boy's eyes such wealth as he had never dreamt of. Rolls of bank notes, priceless jewels, and quantities of money were what he saw. His uncle then besought him not to disgrace the family name by becoming a Christian, and taking his puggaree from his own head he laid it on Sundar's feet, as the last and humblest supplication he could make, with the words, "All these shall be yours if you will remain with us."

Sundar felt this temptation keenly, for not only did the sight of such riches dazzle his eyes, but his heart was deeply moved by his uncle's condescension in thus humiliating himself to the youngest son of the household. Sundar's eyes filled with tears as he beheld the puggaree lying on his feet-marking the disgrace which he must bring on those he loved, and his uncle standing bareheaded before him. But at that moment his heart became filled to overflowing with such love and devotion to Christ that refusal came easily to his lips, and with it came such a sense of divine approbation and acceptance of his dearest Savior as strengthened every holy resolution to be faithful to his Lord. After that his father made it plain to him that he was no longer a son of the house but an outcast.

Both Sundar and a Sikh classmate had read the New Testament with the same result, that they found Christ. But they were not of an age to take the great step of confessing Christ publicly, and so were obliged to remain in their Hindu homes. The relatives of Sundar's friend brought a case into the law courts charging the American missionaries with compelling the boy to become a Christian. Upon appearing before the magistrate the boy bore steady witness to the faith that was in him, and being questioned, he took a New Testament from his pocket and holding it in his hand replied, "Not because of the Padri Sahib but by reading this Injil, I believe on Christ, so let the Padri Sahib go." Thus the case fell through, and for some time longer Sundar and his friend were forced to remain with their relatives until they were able to take the. momentous step that was to mean so much to them both later on.

It is easy to see how, when all persuasion and the temptations of a great career failed to turn aside the boy from his set purpose, the bitterest hostility was aroused amongst his people. His own brother proved his fiercest enemy, and day by day Sundar suffered bitter persecution at his hand. No language was too foul to be used against him and his "Jesus," and with redoubled care he had to steal away where no eye could see him, if he was to refresh his soul by the reading of his precious New Testament. He was taken away from the mission school, which was eventually broken up and had to be closed because of the persecution. Nor was this all, for the open hostility of the villagers became so great that the small Christian community, no longer able to procure food at the shops, was obliged to withdraw to more friendly quarters, leaving Sundar alone and friendless.

As the storm increased in fury Sundar saw that it was impossible for him to remain in his father's house, and so eventually he made his way to the headquarters of the American Presbyterian Mission in Ludhiana, where the missionaries received him kindly and took care of him. Special arrangements were made for the cooking of his food to prevent trouble with his family, and Sundar entered the high school to continue his education. The sensitive boy had high ideals as to what Christians ought to be, and before long he discovered that his school-mates were for the most part only nominally Christian, and the conduct of some of them caused him to leave the mission and retrace his steps homewards. Arrived at Rampur his parents naturally thought he had given up Christianity and received him with great kindness. But they were speedily disillusioned, for they soon found him to be a more determined follower of Jesus than before.

Sundar now took the final step that was to place him hopelessly outside the pale of his religion, community; and family, by cutting short his long hair-the sign to all that he was no longer a Sikh. Sikhs are instructed in their sacred book, the Granth, never to cut the hair, and every true Sikh glories in his hair. Among various races of India the long tuft of hair is regarded with special reverence, and is the last sign of Hinduism a caste man lays aside when he becomes a Christian. So Sundar in cutting his hair brought ostracism on himself, and at the same time it was an unmistakable declaration for Christ and His cross. Then fell on this poor boy the bitterest blow of all. He was to be disowned, cast out, treated only as the lowest of the low, and that by those who loved him best. The Apostle Paul wrote, "We are made as the offscouring [garbage] of all things," and this was the treatment meted out to a boy of sixteen, who up to this point had not entirely cast in his lot with Christians. He was no longer counted as one of the family. His food was served to him outside the house, just as if he belonged to the 'untouchables,' and he was made to sleep in the same place. The first time this was done the poor boy's eyes filled with tears, and the weight of his cross seemed more than he could bear.

Shortly after this, one of Sundar's brothers-in-law, who was in the service of the Raja of Nabha, took him for a day or two to stay at his own house, in the hope of bringing him to a different state of mind. It was then that the Raja heard of the matter, and he summoned Sundar to appear before the bar of the State Assembly (Durbar) to account for his conduct. The Raja used much persuasive language, and made glowing offers to him; moreover he made a stern appeal to his pride of race, reminding him that he was a Singh (lion) and that to be a Christian was to become a dog. Whatever answer Sundar made it must have been given to him in that very hour what he should speak, for neither argument nor appeal nor yet offers of high position were able to move him in his resolution to follow Christ at all costs.

He then returned home, and immediately all the pent-up anger of his father was let loose upon him. The helpless boy was cursed, disowned, and told that on the following morning he must go forth from his ancestral home. With a sorely wounded heart that night he lay down for the last time on his father's verandah to sleep. Before sunrise the following day he was cast forth with nothing but the thin clothes he wore, and enough money to take him to Patiala by rail. Homeless, friendless, and utterly destitute, Sundar turned his back on the home of his childhood.

> Jesus, I my cross have taken,
> All to leave and follow Thee;
> Destitute, despised, forsaken,
> Thou from hence my All shalt be.

Chapter 8
Called To Suffer-2

"Thou art called, and hast professed a good confession before many witnesses."- 1 Timothy 6:12.

As Sundar sat in the train the thought came to him that in Ropur there was a little colony of Christians- some from Rampur, whither they had fled when persecution made life impossible in their own village-and so stepping out of the train he made his way to the house of the kind Indian pastor and his good wife. It was by the providence of God that Sundar did this, for very soon after his arrival he fell violently ill and a physician had to be called in. Then it became known that a deadly poison had been mixed in the food given him before leaving home. It was not the intention of his friends that they should be degraded in the eyes of the world, but rather that he should die in the train. All that night the good pastor's wife sat by his side waiting for the end to come, for the physician pronounced the case hopeless and departed with the promise to come in the morning to the funeral.

Sundar lay in mortal pain with blood flowing from his mouth and his strength ebbing fast. But as he lay, there came to him the profound belief that God had not called him out of darkness to die without witnessing to his faith in Christ, so he began to pray with all his remaining powers. When morning came he was still alive, though exceedingly weak. The physician came according to his promise and was amazed to find the boy alive. So deeply impressed was he that he took a copy of the New Testament and began to study it. In this way the physician himself became a believer in Christ, and today is working as a missionary in Burma.

Sundar's friend, in taking the same step, received similar treatment, for his relatives also offered him poisoned food to eat. While Sundar lay between life and death his friend's short but heroic witness to the power of Christ came to an end, and he passed to the presence of his Redeemer to be "forever with the Lord."

When Sundar was sufficiently strong to undertake the short journey to Ludhiana he went back to the kind care of the American missionaries there. While there several attempts were made by his relatives to get him away, and violence was used on one of these occasions, so that the police had to be called in to quell the disturbance. But the most trying occurrence to Sundar was when his aged father came to make a last appeal in the hope of drawing him away. The sight of the father's stricken face and figure made a deep impression on the boy, and as the old man spoke of the great love of his mother and happy days of his childhood, there passed in fleeting panorama before Sundar's mind all the happiness of his old home, and the love that had sheltered his early days. His tears scorched his cheeks, while a mighty struggle went on in his heart. But he was not left to struggle alone, for One stood by him and reinforced his soul's resolve to take up his cross and follow Him. As his father turned to go away the last great sacrifice was made, and Sundar stood as he does today-stripped of all that life can offer but accepted of his Lord. These long months, so full of trial and hardship, had been a supreme test, and every fresh sorrow only added sweetness and firmness to the character of this remarkable boy.

After these events it became necessary for Sundar to go away where he would be protected from his enemies, and he was sent to the American Medical Mission at Sabathu, a small place twenty-three miles from Simla, where he was free from persecution, and able to give his mind completely to the study of his beloved New Testament. Set free from all earth's ties, he became increasingly anxious to confess Christ by baptism. Again and again he begged that he might be allowed to take this step, and eventually on his birthday, September 3, 1905, the Rev. J. Redman baptized him in the Church of England at Simla. Next day Sundar returned to Sabathu, and knowing that he was "buried with Him in baptism . . . risen with Him through faith" (Col. ii. 12) his heart was filled to overflowing with happiness. The weary struggles of the past months faded in the presence of this new joy of bearing the name of the dear Master for whom already he had suffered so much.

His heart now became filled with a burning desire to make known to others the Savior to whom he had given himself so unreservedly, and with eager joy he began to look forward to the great work to which his life was to be dedicated. During the hard days of his search after God Sundar had made a vow that if God would lead him into peace he would sacrifice all that life could offer him. And now the day had come when he could make an utter self-surrender for Jesus Christ. He had long felt drawn to the life of a sadhu, and knowing what' such a life involved, he willingly made the final sacrifice for it. His books and personal belongings were soon disposed of, and on October 6, 1905, just thirty-three days after his baptism, he adopted the simple saffron robe that was to mark him off for all time as one vowed to a religious life. With bare feet and no visible means of support, but with his New Testament in is hand and his Lord at his side, Sadu Sundar Singh set out on the evangelistic campaign that has lasted to this day.

Chapter 9
Called To Serve

"It pleased God who . . . called me by His grace to reveal His Son in me, that I might preach Him among the heathen."- Galatians 1:15-16.

"Ye shall be witnesses unto Me ... in Jerusalem."- Acts 1:8.

Sundar was now embarked on a life of such complete self-abnegation and suffering as falls to the lot of few men in this world. His path from Hinduism to Christ had been one of thorns all the way. But, after his vision of the thorn-crowned Jesus and his acceptance of the peace his Savior brought, nothing seemed too great to give up for Him. In the undying words of Dr. Watts:-

Were the whole realm of nature mine,
That were an offering far too small;
Love so amazing, so divine,
Demands my soul, my life, my all.

Nothing less than 'all sufficed to satisfy his ardent nature, and one cannot wonder that on entering the sadhu life in that spirit he determined, as he says, that "His grace abiding" he would live no other, so long as life was his to spend for Christ.

Though but a boy in years, the heart of Sadhu Sundar Singh then, as now, was filled with a divine passion for human souls, and his intense devotion and love for the Lord Jesus caused him to choose as his first field of labor his own village, from which he had been driven only a short time previously. Only a few months after his rejection by his family the young Sadhu returned to the familiar streets of Rampur, and there in every street he bore faithful witness to the power of the Savior and the new-found happiness he had in Him. Not only so, but even the zanana doors of Rampur were opened to him, and he went from house to house telling the women the same wonderful story. From there, and alone, he passed on to the villages round about, and fearlessly testified to the people everywhere of the great peace only obtainable through Jesus Christ.

He then continued his way through many other towns and villages of the Punjab, working his way up towards Afghanistan and Kashmir. This was a long and extremely arduous tour, and, unused to the hardships of sadhu life, Sundar suffered severely from the cold and privations of the way. Moreover the work was difficult, for his message met with little response. It was however at the ancient city of Jalalabad in Afghanistan that he met some Pathans [ethnic Afghans], who, planning his destruction, were eventually willing to receive his message. An account of this will be found in a later chapter.

Up to this point it seems as if God had, little by little, weaned Sundar from all that life holds dear. Relatives, wealth, home, had all gone for Christ. Entering the new world of Christians the comfort and almost certain preferment that would have been his, were to count for naught to him who had set out on his first tour to make Christ known in the heathen villages amongst the mountains. The cold pierced his thin clothing, the thorns and stones cut his bare feet. The nights came with no certainty of shelter from the bitter winds and pouring rain, and the grey dawn often brought days of hunger and suffering such as he had never known. Even his fervent soul quailed at the hardship that seemed to bring so little return, for often his message was discredited and he himself cast forth to spend a hungry night in caves or any poor shelter the jungle might afford. His sadhu's clothes gave him entrance everywhere, but often when it was discovered that he was a Christian, Sundar was driven hungry and helpless from the villages to live or die.

But nothing can discourage him. Incapable of drawing back in face of danger or death itself, Sadhu Sundar Singh continues his sublime mission in the darkest corners' of India and the regions beyond. Year in and out he has labored for the souls of men in plain and mountain, in city and village, and amongst the scattered peoples and wandering tribes on the frontiers of India. It has been amongst these peoples that he has suffered so severely, but amongst them too he has had the supreme joy not only of making Christ known, but of leading men to His feet. His chief work has been done amongst non-Christians, to whom he feels God's call to be clear and unmistakable.

Chapter 10
Called To Preach

"For I determined not to know anything among you, save Jesus Christ, and Him crucified."- 1 Corinthians 2:2.

Very weary after his long and hard journey through the Punjab, Kashmir, Baluchistan and Afghanistan, the Sadhu retraced his steps and came to Kotgarh, a small place beyond Simla in the Himalayas, where he remained a time for rest. This little place will always be associated with Sundar Singh, for early in his career he labored there, and it is to Kotgarh still that he retires for a brief rest between his tours, or before starting on his arduous journeys into the closed lands of Tibet and Nepal.

During the summer of 1906, Sundar met Mr. Stokes, who was staying near Ketgarh. This wealthy American gentleman had come to India to labor for her people, and for the glory of God. Meeting the Sadhu fired his heart, and filled him with a desire to join him in his arduous life. After prayer and thought Mr. Stokes took this step, and the two Sadhus took a journey together through the Khangra valley.

Food and shelter were difficult to obtain, and the two brothers suffered much, but their work was good and their fellowship sweet. It was during this journey that Sundar Singh fell ill. The two Sadhus had travelled together for some hundreds of miles, sharing the same hardships, often being obliged to seek shelter in the common filthy serais, and often subsisting on the barest and roughest diet, and little enough of that. They were passing through very unhealthy country when Sundar was seized with fever and severe internal pains. Shaking with ague, burning with fever and always in pain, he dragged on until at last he could walk no longer. He sank on the .path almost unconscious, and Mr. Stokes moved him into an easier position, enquiring at the same time as to how he was. No complaint ever passes the lips of the Sadhu whatever his lot, and Mr. Stokes was not at all surprised to receive the reply he did. With a smile, though in a feeble voice, the Sadhu answered, "I am very happy. How sweet it is to suffer for His sake." Those who know the Sadhu best know that "this is the key-note of his life."

It was a wild and jungly place where this happened, and Mr. Stokes was in great difficulty, but he succeeded in getting the sick man to the house of a European some miles away, where he was nursed to health again. The kind host was at that time without any care for religion, but day by day he saw the example of the Sadhu and heard such things from his lips as caused him to think deeply, until he became a truly converted man. Thus was this illness blessed to the saving of one soul who found joy and peace in Christ Jesus.

Mr. Stokes possessed a magic lantern which the Sadhu borrowed and used in Rampur and other places for street preaching at night, when large numbers of people gathered to see the pictures and hear the explanation. Thus unweariedly, night and day, the two Sadhus passed from place to place, doing most of their travelling by night, because the sun was too fierce for Mr. Stokes to bear its rays on his unprotected head. It was at this time that Mr. Stokes spoke so appreciatively of the work of the Sadhu, who, though not much more than a boy, was so filled with his message that wherever he went people were under a strange compulsion to listen to what he said.

In 1907 the two Sadhus labored in the Leper Asylum at Sabathu, and later in the year they went down to Lahore to work amongst the plague-stricken in the Plague Camp there. They toiled unremittingly day and night, allowing themselves only brief hours of respite, and even these were spent lying on the ground amongst the sick and dying.

The next year Mr. Stokes went to America on furlough and Sundar was once more left alone. From Lahore he went on to Sindh, returning through Rajputana to North India again, and then as the hot weather drew on he made his first journey into the closed land of Tibet. In all these places the Gospel was preached incessantly, and no man who came across the Sadhu went away without hearing that Jesus had come into the world to save sinners.

After his return from Tibet he had a great desire to go to Palestine, in the belief that to see the place where his Savior had lived and died would inspire him to fuller and better service. But when he reached Bombay he found it impracticable, so in 1909 he returned to North India through the Central Provinces, preaching as he went.

Chapter 11
What Wisdom Is This?

"From whence hath this Man these things? and what wisdom
is this which is given unto Him . . . ? -- Mark 6:2.

That Sundar Singh was taught of God was unmistakably
shown by the wonderful hearing he got amongst non-Christians
thus early in his career. His friends recognized that he possessed
unusual powers, and that his presentation of the Gospel held people by its attractiveness and persuasiveness. So much was this the
case that they felt it desirable to widen the sphere of his operations by including the Christian community among those to
whom he went. But for this some definite preparation was needed, and they advised him to join the St. John's Divinity College,
Lahore. This he did, passing on entry the examination usually im-
posed at the close of the first year, and proceeding at once to the
second year's course. The years 1909 and 1910 were spent in
study, and during vacation time he continued his evangelistic
work as heretofore.

Sundar still wore the saffron robe. The sadhu idea for a Christian was something quite new at that time, and was a cause of
considerable doubt to many. But he never swerved from his first
resolution, although the criticism he was often subjected to, tend-
ed to make these years hard for him.

While Sundar was in college Mr. Stokes returned from furlough, having gone to England and there started the idea of a
brotherhood, whose work should be exclusively for the glory of
God and the help of man, in whatever form it might present itself-

not necessarily the work of preaching. The humbler and harder the labors, the better! The Archbishop of Canterbury was approached on the matter, and seemed to think it would be a good thing, so that after Mr. Stokes returned to India this brotherhood was started with five persons, the only Indian being the Sadhu. The brotherhood was inaugurated in a solemn service in Lahore Cathedral, when two of the five took the vows, but Sundar remained a novice, having already vowed himself to the life of a sadhu for Christ's sake.

Upon leaving college he was recommended for deacon's orders by the Diocesan Mission Council and was granted a license to preach. Soon after leaving college his heart turned to Tibet, whither he went for the six months of hot weather, returning to Kotgarh, where he worked in connexion with the Church Missionary Society for some time.

Like the great English preacher, John Wesley, the Sadhu looked upon the world as his parish, and he preached everywhere and to all who would give heed to his message. It was not long before dissatisfaction was expressed at his methods of work. He was told that in deacon's orders it was undesirable, and that as a priest it would be impossible, to continue working in this way. The pure and simple spirit of the man never for a moment staggered or stayed to contemplate what would be the result if he declined to obey. The sheltered life of a priest with its possibilities of preferment held no temptation for Sundar. On his knees and in the quiet of his own spirit he settled the momentous question, and then took the step that forever set him free of all sects. He returned his license to preach, to his Bishop, explaining that he felt called to preach to all, and wherever God sent him. Bishop Lefroy (late Metropolitan of India), with a generous large-heartedness, accepted the reason with the license.

The great crisis of his career was safely past. From that day Sadhu Sundar Singh made himself the possession of Christians of all creeds, and also set himself free for a mighty work amongst nonChristians all over India.

Chapter 12
Early Experiences As A Sadhu

"He which converteth a sinner from the error of his way shall save a soul from death, and shall hide a multitude of sins."-James 5:20.

"Joy shall be in heaven over one sinner that repenteth."- Luke 15:7.

The years 1911 and 1912 were spent in touring in Garhwal, Nepal, Kulu, the Punjab, and many other places, while each year during the six months of hot weather the Sadhu went alone to Tibet. The following incidents give some idea of his life and work at that time. Sundar Singh was one day making his way to a certain village when he caught sight of two men in front of him, one of whom suddenly disappeared. A little further on he overtook the remaining man, who accosted him, and pointing to a sheeted figure on the ground told the Sadhu that this was his friend who had died by the way, and he had no money to bury him. Sundar had only his blanket and two pice [less than one cent value] which had been given him for the toll bar, but these he gave to the man and passed on his way. He had not gone far when the man came running after him, and sobbed out that his companion was really dead. The Sadhu did not understand, until he began to explain that it was their custom to take it in turns to prey on the public by pretending one of them was dead.

This they had done for years, but that day when the man went back to call his friend there was no response, and on lifting the cloth he was horror-stricken to find him actually dead. The

wretched man sought the Sadhu's forgiveness, being assured that
here was some great saint whom he had robbed of all he had, and
thus had the dire displeasure of the gods fallen upon them. Then
Sundar spoke to him of the Lord of life, and in that penitent moment the man accepted the message. He sent him to a mission station near Garhwal, where in due time he was baptized.

On one of his long journeys in the mountains the footpath divided at a certain point, and he was in doubt as to which path to
take. He chose the wrong one, and upon arrival at a village he
found he had gone eleven miles out of his way. Turning back
Sundar met a man with whom he entered into conversation, and
began to speak to him of Christ. Then the man produced from the
folds of his clothes a copy of the New Testament, which he confessed to having hid when he saw the Sadhu coming, in the belief
that he was a Hindu sanyasi. The man had doubts to which he
could find no solution, but Sundar so dealt with them that the man
found Christ. In speaking of this to the writer, Sundar remarked:
"Then I knew why I had gone astray, for Christ had sent me to
help this anxious soul."

At Narkanda the Sadhu found some men reaping in a field.
Joining them he spoke to them, as they worked, of Jesus and eternal things. At first they listened with indifference and then with
disapprobation. They had no mind to hear about a strange religion.
Some of the men began to curse and threaten him, and one took a
stone and hit him on the head. After a time the man who had
thrown the stone was seized with a severe headache and had to
stop work. The Sadhu then took up the scythe and reaped with the
others. This softened their hearts and at the end of the day the men
invited him to accompany them home. In the quiet of the evening
a better opportunity was afforded for the giving of his message,
and then he went away. The reapers, having rested, began to take
stock of the harvest gathered that day, and to their astonishment
found a greater yield than they had had in previous years. They
were then afraid, and declared amongst themselves that a holy
man had visited them and this increase was proof of it. Then they
strove to find the Sadhu, that they might give better heed to his

message, but found him nowhere.

This incident was published in a North Indian paper, The Nur Afghan, by one of the men present on the occasion, who made an appeal through its pages to Sundar to return amongst them that they might receive his message.

At the ancient city of Jalalabad the Sadhu found himself amongst a cruel and treacherous people, who seeing he was a Christian laid a plot to take his life. Sitting to rest himself, the news was brought to him by one less evil-disposed than the rest, but as he had done nothing to warrant such a thing he, found it difficult to believe it possible. However, he decided to take the warning and to seek a safer retreat. Only the common serai, infested with mosquitoes and viler insects remained, so to this he went. Next morning, when he had lit a fire and was drying his wet clothes, a number of Pathans [ethnic Afghans] arrived. Much to his amazement the foremost of these men came in and fell at his feet. The Pathan then explained how they had sought to take his life, but seeing him had altered their intention, for instead of his being frozen as they had expected, he was well and none the worse for his experiences. They were driven to believe that here was one favored of Allah, and they begged that he would accept of their hospitality and accompany them home. The Sadhu spent a very happy week with them, and they gave good heed to his teaching, so that he believes there will be fruit of his labors amongst these rough and hardened men.

Chapter 13
Obedience By Suffering

"Yet learned He obedience by the things which He suffered."-
Hebrews 5:8.

"I count all things but loss . . . that I may know Him . . . and
the fellowship of His suffering."- Phil. 3:8, 10.

No one but Sadhu Similar Singh' himself knows how great
have been his sufferings during his years of service for his Master.
He admits that very often he has gone without proper food, being
reduced to eating the berries and produce of the jungle, and many
a night he has been driven from the villages and been obliged to
sleep under trees or in caves of the earth. The parts of India where
the chief of his work has been done are no places for such a life, so
that it is not surprising that on more than one occasion the Sadhu
has shared his miserable shelter with a snake or wild animal.

At a village in the district of Thoria the people behaved so badly to him that his nights were always spent in the jungle as long as
he was working amongst them. On a particularly dark night, after
a discouragingly hard day, the Sadhu found a cave where he
spread his blanket and lay down to sleep. When daylight came it
revealed the horrible spectacle of a large leopard still asleep close
to him. The sight almost paralyzed him with fear, but once outside
the cave he could only reflect upon the great providence of God
that had preserved him while he slept. His own words are: "Never
to this day has any wild animal done me any harm."

On another occasion, being driven out of a certain village,
Sundar went to meditate on a rock close to a cave. Deep in con-

templation, it was some time before he noticed that he was being stealthily observed by a black panther that was crouching not far away. Filled with fear but putting his trust in God, he quietly rose and walked forward as if nothing were there. He got away safely to the village, and when the people knew of his escape they declared he must be a very holy man, since this very panther had killed several people from that village. They then gathered round to receive the message which they had spurned before, and so Sundar again thanked God and took courage.

One morning a number of sadhus were gathered on the banks of the Ganges at a place called Kishi Kesh amidst a crowd of religious bathers, and amongst them stood Sadhu Sundar Singh, Testament in hand, preaching. Some were listening in a mildly interested way, while others joked and scoffed at the man and his message. Unexpectedly a man from the crowd lifted up a handful of sand and threw it in his eyes, ah act that roused the indignation of a better-disposed man, who handed the offender over to a policeman. Meanwhile the Sadhu went down to the river and washed the sand from his eyes. Upon his return he begged for the release of the culprit and proceeded with his preaching. Surprised by this act and the way he had taken the insult, the man, Vidyananda, fell at his feet begging his forgiveness, and declaring a desire to understand more of what the Sadhu was speaking about. This man became a seeker after truth, and afterwards accompanied him on his journey, learning with meekness from his lips the story of redeeming love.

Very early in his pilgrimages Sundar travelled through a number of villages, one of which was called Doliwahi. The day had been a hard one, the march very long, and the Sadhu arrived utterly exhausted and badly in need of food and rest. Walking down the village street he asked again and again for some shelter where he might spend the night, but in every place- when it was discovered that he was a Christian- he was driven away. Heavy rain was falling and it was bitterly cold. Wearied almost to death, Sundar sought refuge in a ruined hut of two rooms, without doors or windows. At least he was out of the rain, and thanking God he laid his blanket in the driest spot and went hungry to bed.

Soon he fell asleep, and did not wake until the chilly grey dawn came. In the half-darkness he saw a black object coiled up in his blanket close beside him, and looking closer he discovered that a huge cobra had also sought shelter and warmth beside him. Speedily he escaped from the hut, leaving the snake asleep, but on further thought he returned. Seizing a corner of the blanket he shook it free of the venomous reptile, which sluggishly wriggled off to the furthest corner of the room. Sundar then took his blanket with a feeling of great thankfulness that God had taken care of him in the hours of sleep, and. spared him for further service.

An educated Arya Samaj gentleman relates how one day when he was descending a mountain he met a young Sadhu going up. Curiosity prompted him to watch what would happen, so instead of joining him for a talk as he at first thought of doing, he waited, and this was what he saw. When the Sadhu got to the village he sat down upon a log, and wiping the perspiration from his face he commenced singing a Christian hymn. Soon a crowd gathered, but when it was found that the love of Christ was the theme many of the people became angry. One man jumped up and dealt him such a severe blow as felled him to the ground, cutting his cheek and hand badly. Without a word Sundar rose and bound up his bleeding hand, and with blood running down his face prayed for his enemies and spoke to them of the forgiving love of Christ. In writing of this incident this gentleman adds that he himself, by seeing the Sadhu's conduct, was "drawn out of the well of contempt, and brought to the fountain of life." The man, Kripa Ram, who had thrown Sundar down, sought long and earnestly for him, in the hope that he might be baptized by "that wounded hand," but not finding him, he openly confessed Christ by baptism, and still hopes to see Sadhu Sundar Singh someday.

Chapter 14
The Fast

"When thou prayest . . . pray to thy Father which is in secret."- Matthew 6:6.

"When thou fastest . . . appear not unto men to fast, but to thy Father, which is in secret."- Matthew 6:17, 18.

Towards the end of 1912 a letter was received by the Rev. Canon Sandys of Calcutta, from Canada, asking for --

"A Christian Sikh to be sent as a preacher to work amongst 4000 Sikh lumbermen in British Columbia. The request was laid before Sundar Singh, who at once agreed to go. . . . Everything was ready for him, when the shipping agents declined to send him, on the ground that the Canadian Government had passed immigration laws which made it impossible for them to book him through." Sundar Singh felt the disappointment keenly, but simply said, "'Perhaps it is not God's will I should ever go to Canada."

Later Canon Sandys wrote, "I failed to get a passport for him, as the Government no doubt was at that time receiving private information about the Columbian Sikhs." And so to the Sadhu's sorrow the idea had to be abandoned.

He then worked his way across the country from Calcutta to Bombay, and eventually north again. After his baptism he had two strong desires, one being to visit Palestine, the scene of our Savior's life and work, and the other to imitate Jesus in fasting forty days and forty nights. By these means he hoped to obtain fresh spiritual" enlightenment. To achieve the first in 1908 he made his way to Bombay, but found that for various reasons the journey at that time was impracticable. Some four years later, when the proposed visit to Canada fell through, the Sadhu's mind turned to the idea of retirement for prayer and fasting, in the belief that these things would minister to the great need for a closer communion with God and increased power for service.

It was about this time that he came in contact with a Roman Catholic medical man, a Franciscan, calling himself Dr. Swift, and travelling with him up north they discussed the idea of a fast, the latter striving to dissuade the Sadhu from attempting it, and declaring that death would surely result if he did. Seeing, however, that he still desired to accomplish it, the Doctor begged him to give him the addresses of his chief friends, that in case of necessity he might communicate with them.

This was done and the two men parted, the Doctor with the intention of joining a Catholic fraternity, and the Sadhu with the determination to seek retirement that he might give himself to fasting and prayer. The Doctor wrote to a friend of his near Dehra Dun telling him of what was happening, while away in the jungly country between Hardwar and Dehra Dun, Sundar Singh went alone to meet his God.

The days passed without any news of him filtering through to the outside world, and meanwhile he remained in the jungle without food, and growing weaker every day. Having been warned as to what might happen to him the Sadhu made provision for increasing weakness by collecting forty stones, one of which he dropped each day in order to keep the count, but at length he was unable even to do this. His hearing and sight left him and he lay as one in a trance, conscious of what was going on about him but unable to make any outward sign of life. As physical powers declined and extreme exhaustion set in he felt within himself a great quickening of the spirit, and in this state his complete dependence upon God, and other matters of intense spiritual importance, were revealed to him, so that since that time none of the doubts that once assailed him have had any power over him. In this condition he was found by some bamboo-cutters who, seeing his saffron robe, lifted him into his blanket, and conveyed him to Rishi Kesh and then to Dehra Dun. From there he was sent in a carriage to Annfield. So altered was he in appearance by what he had passed through that he was not recognized by his Christian friends at Annfield. But they knew who he was by the name in his Testament, and carefully nursed him back to life.

Meanwhile Dr. Swift received news from his friend that a man corresponding to his description of the Sadhu had been discovered in the jungle at the point of death. Surmising that his predictions had come true the Doctor (possibly through a friend) wired to the Sadhu's friends that "Sundar Singh slept in Jesus." The Metropolitan and Canon Sandys were two of the six who received these telegrams. The latter wrote to the station master from whence the telegrams had been sent, making enquiries as to who the sender was, and the reply came that they had been handed in "by a black-coated gentleman."

While Sundar was lying weak and ill at Annfield, unconscious of the reports being circulated about him, obituaries appeared in the papers, and a memorial service was held in the church at Simla, money also being contributed for a tablet to be placed there in his memory. By March he was well enough to resume his travels, and went up to Simla, when he heard the story of his reported death.

This fearful experience did bring the spiritual enlightenment the Sadhu had believed it would, and although count of time was lost, and the fast could not have lasted for forty days, this enlightenment was gained almost at the loss of his life.

Chapter 15
Further Journeys And Persecutions

"Christ shall be magnified in my body, whether it be |by life or by death."- Phil. 1:20.

After his recovery from the effects of the fast, Sadhu Similar Singh went again to Tibet for the six months of the hot weather of 1913, and returning spent the cold season touring through North India. Early the following year he was again in Bengal, and working his way up to Darjeeling he entered Sikkim. The Native States bordering Northern India, chief of which are Nepal, Sikkim, and Bhutan, are ruled by princes of their own, and are as hostile to Christianity as Tibet itself. The people are superstitious and ignorant, and the preaching of a foreign religion is strictly prohibited within certain areas. In 191+ Sadhu Sundar Singh entered Nepal knowing that he ran every risk of ill-treatment and possibly death. For some time, however, in spite of opposition and threats, he went from place to place publishing the good news until he came to a town called Ilom. He had not been there long when he was told he must discontinue preaching or some evil would befall him.

An order was issued for his imprisonment, and while delivering his message he was seized and hurried off to the common prison, to spend his days and nights with murderers and thieves. Here was an opportunity for him to speak for his Master, and soon he began to tell the unhappy prisoners of the power of Christ to change men's hearts and to bring peace to their consciences even within the dismal walls of a prison. Many believed his message of joy and accepted Christ, and thus were these fearful days converted into seasons of blessing both to the Sadhu and to those whom he taught.

The news that he was changing the hearts of his fellow-prisoners was told in high places, and on this charge Sundar was removed from the prison and taken to the public market for punishment. Here he was stripped of his clothes and made to sit on the bare earth. His feet and hands were fastened into holes in upright boards (stocks), and in this crippled position, without food or water, he was made to remain all day and the following night. To add to his tortures a number of leeches were thrown over his naked body, and these immediately fastened upon him and began to suck his life-blood. He carries the marks of this horrible treatment today, so that of him it may be truly said, "I bear in my body the marks of the Lord Jesus." A mocking crowd stood round to watch his torture, and none offered him even a drink of water to relieve his physical misery. In speaking of this experience to the writer the Sadhu said, "I do not know how it was, but my heart was so full of joy I could not help singing and preaching."

Through the long night he agonized, growing hourly weaker with loss of blood, but when morning came he was still alive. When his persecutors saw the Sadhu's tranquil face they were filled with superstitious dread, and being sure that he held some strange power they did not understand, they took him out of the stocks and set him free. This dreadful experience had made him so weak that he fell unconscious, and only after some time and many attempts did he manage to crawl away from the spot. In that place were some secret believers belonging to the Sanyasi Mission (spoken of in a later chapter) and these kind people received their wounded brother and cared for him until strength returned.

The Sadhu's brief record of his days in the prison of Ilom will be found in a later chapter, and, as in his case it is to be expected, he ascribes his great joy in that dreary place to the near companionship of his never-failing Friend, Jesus Christ.

At Srinagar in Garhwal, he had a most unexpected experience. He knew that this was a dangerous place in which to speak of Christ, but one day when he was preaching outside the city some young men taunted him by saying he dare not say such things inside the city. He felt impelled to accept the challenge, and entering the city he went to the market place and there started to preach. Upon seeing this some of the bystanders hurried off to bring the pandit [scholar and teacher] of the place, hoping he would controvert the Sadhu's statements and put him to shame.

When the pandit arrived he went up to Sundar, and in front of all the people he placed his two forefingers in the Sadhu's mouth with the words, "I have done this to prove that we are brothers, and not enemies as you suppose, for we both believe in Jesus Christ as Savior." The effect upon the crowd was electrical, and before many minutes had passed all his enemies had vanished away. Sundar then passed one of the happiest days of his life in conversation with this good man, discovering, much to his joy, that the pandit only prolonged his stay in that dark place in order to bring others to the light. Already he had by God's grace secretly won sixteen souls, and intended to carry on this work so long as it was God's will he should.

In the wild and inhospitable regions which Sadhu Sundar Singh often needs to pass through in the course of his missionary journeys, he naturally has varied and often most extraordinary experiences. One such occurred when he was passing through the thickly wooded forests of Bhulera, which is a favorite haunt of thieves and murderers. Four men suddenly intercepted him and one rushed on him with a drawn knife. Unable to protect himself, and believing the end had come, he bowed his head to receive the blow. This unexpected conduct caused the man to hesitate, and to ask instead that the Sadhu should hand over all he had. He was searched for money, but finding none his blanket was seized and he was allowed to pursue his way.

Thankful to escape with his life he went on, but before he had gone far one of them called to him to return, and now certain that death awaited him he turned back. The man then enquired who he was and what was his teaching. Sundar told him that he was a

Christian Sadhu, and opening his Testament he read to him the story of the rich man and Lazarus. The man listened attentively, and in reply to the question as to what were his thoughts, he replied that the end of the rich man had filled him with dread, adding that if such a terrible punishment followed so small a sin what would become of greater sinners.

The opportunity thus afforded was quickly seized by the Sadhu. He immediately opened up the riches of God's grace to him, and listening, the man's heart was deeply moved. He poured out a miserable story of guilt and sin, amidst many sobs and tears. He then took Sundar to his cave, prepared food for him, and begged him to eat. After some more conversation and a short prayer, the two men retired to rest. Very early next morning the man awoke Sundar and, bringing him outside took him, to a cave where there was a ghastly heap of human bones. With loud weeping he pointed to the bones and said, "These are my sins; tell me, is there any hope for such as me?" The Sadhu's heart was touched by the man's anxiety and contrition, and he told him of the thief who was forgiven on the cross. Then they knelt together and the poor sinner sobbed out his repentance to God. Before the Sadhu had finished with him, the man had made a start on the strait and narrow way, and together they went to Labeha, Sakkum, where he was handed over to the missionaries and eventually baptized. The other three men also gave up their bad life and took to honest occupations. Thus was the Sadhu used for the help of four great sinners.

Chapter 16
Tibet

The Chumbi valley on the northern side of Darjeeling is an indescribably lovely and seductive spot, and is one of the approaches to the barest and most inhospitable country of Asia-Tibet.

Tibet has not always been a closed land. Until the end of the eighteenth century only physical obstacles stood in the way of entry into Lhasa itself. Jesuits and Capuchins reached Lhasa and made long stays there, and were even encouraged by the Tibetan government. As early as 1325 it is known that foreigners visited the country, but the first Europeans to reside in Lhasa arrived there in 1661.

Two centuries ago Europeans might travel in remote parts of Asia with greater safety than is possible today, for now the white man inspires fear where he used only to awaken curiosity. At the end of the eighteenth century the Nepalese overran Tibet, and the Chinese being called in to aid, almost annihilated the Gurkhas. From that time China practically ruled in Lhasa. The policy of strict exclusion dates from then. Since the decline of China's power, a Tibetan Mission to the Czar, supposedly of a religious character, brought Tibet somewhat under the influence of Russia. Several Buriat lamas had been educated in Russia, chief of whom was one Dorjieff, who headed the Russo-Tibetan Mission of 1901. Dorjieff and others inspired dreams of a consolidated Buddhist religion, under the spiritual control of the Dalai Lama, backed by the military power of Russia; this was believed possible because the ignorant lamas imagined Russia to be a Buddhist country.

Tibet is a mysterious country with an ancient but arrested civilization; a land where prayer flags flutter in the wind, and where men spend' half their time in turning mechanical prayer wheels. The people are mediaeval in government. Witchcraft, incantations, and ordeals by fire and boiling are still common. The entire population is only about six millions.

In Lhasa, the home of the Buddha and the Dalai Lama, is a superbly detached building on a hill of rock called the Potala. "Its massive walls, its terraces and bastions stretch upward from the plain to the crest, and are crowned with glittering domes shining with turquoise and gold. At its feet lies the squalid city of Lhasa. Buddhism holds all life sacred, yet this place, where dwells the divine incarnation, has witnessed more murder than even the bloodstained castles of mediaeval Europe."

The Buddhist religion is the one thing that keeps the nation together, and every family must contribute one son to the priestly order of Lamas. Hundreds of years ago a Buddhist saint predicted that Tibet would one day be invaded and conquered, and Buddhism would become extinct. Thus it is that a blind fear and fanaticism combine to keep all doors of entrance closed to this land, and the teaching of a foreign religion more than anything else brings down on the head of the offender the severest persecution, and even the most cruel death.

Chapter 17
Sundar in Tibet

"When I came ... to preach Christ's gospel, a door was opened unto me of the Lord" (2 Cor. ii. 12) ... a great door . . . and there are many adversaries."-1 Cor. 16:9.

"Their feet are swift to shed blood . . . and the way of peace have they not known."-Romans 3:15-17.

Born and bred in the far north and familiar with the mountainous regions of the Himalayas, Sundar's heart turned to the dark places where no vision of Christ has come.

Feeling as he does about Christ it is not surprising that he eventually made choice of the most difficult and dangerous fields "where Christ is not named" as his peculiar sphere. It therefore seems quite a natural thing that the mind of Sadhu Sundar Singh should have turned to the closed land of Tibet soon after he set out to preach the Gospel. For more than a century the vast continent of India had had its missionaries, and hundreds of thousands of India's children had responded to the call of Christ, many of whom in their turn had become messengers of peace to their own people. In his own words, " There are many to proclaim the truth in India," but as he turned towards Tibet and the contiguous country of Nepal, his heart went out to the people who have no means of hearing of Christ.

Foreign missionaries are debarred from entering the country, and it is scarcely easier for an Indian, for he must not only face the inhospitality of the bitter climate, but the active hostility of a half-civilized and wholly fanatical people. But to suffer for the Master's sake has been a great mark of the life of Sadhu Sundar Singh, and so, undismayed by what probably lay before him, he set out while still a boy on his first journey into that land of bigotry and darkness.

> Christ the Son of God hath sent me
> Through the midnight lands,
> Mine the mighty ordination
> Of the pierced hands.

Unfortunately the Sadhu has not kept any connected account of his work and journeys through Tibet, so that all there is to tell is in the shape of fragments of his experiences, sufferings, and successes in that fascinating and yet terrible land.

On his first journey in 1908, when he was scarcely nineteen years of age, he started alone and was unacquainted with the language spoken in Tibet. He was very glad to avail himself of the help offered to him by two Moravian missionaries working at Poo, a little frontier town. He stayed a week with these good men, and then they gave him a worker of their own who was to accompany him for some distance, and instruct him in the dialect of the people. Except that he knew the intense hostility of the Tibetans to every religion but their own, the Sadhu had little knowledge of place or people, but it was not long that he remained in ignorance.

He soon found they resented his teaching, and wherever he went he was met with bitter opposition and hatred, especially from the Lamas. These men were particularly venomous, and often assumed a threatening attitude on the border of the crowds that gathered to hear his preaching. Notwithstanding this, he reached the important town of Tashigang in safety, and was astonished and pleased to receive kindly treatment at the hands of the head Lama of the place. This man was a person of importance, and under him served some hundreds of inferior lamas.

The Lama not only received the Sadhu with kindness but provided him with food and shelter, and as the weather was bitterly cold this hospitality was most acceptable. Moreover the Lama called a gathering of those under his control to hear the Sadhu's message, and so the Gospel was preached by him with great thankfulness of heart.

Journeying on from this place he was fortunate enough to arrive at a town under the rule of another Lama who was a friend of the Lama of Tashigang, and here again he was accorded a welcome and a good hearing. From this place he visited several other towns and villages, but in these he met with even greater opposition than in his earlier work. He was constantly threatened and warned to get out of the country lest some evil befall him. But he was not to be thus terrorized, and he continued his work amidst many difficulties.

Thus has Sadhu Sundar Singh "besieged this stronghold of bigotry and fanaticism," and in doing so has passed through many tribulations; but to him persecution and infamy are as nothing if he may win but one soul for his Savior. A Ceylon friend says, "His resolution to walk barefooted amidst the perpetual snows of Tibet is the mark of his invincible determination to bring men to Christ."

Chapter 18
Sundar In Tibet- 2

"For the work of Christ he was nigh unto death, not regarding his life."-Phil. 2:30.

"I am ready not to be bound only, but also to die . . . for the name of the Lord Jesus."- Acts 21:13.

With a deep determination to make the name of Christ known in this hostile country the Sadhu continued his work, knowing that sooner or later bitter persecution would be his lot. At a town called Rasar he was arrested and arraigned before the head Lama on the charge of entering the country and preaching the Gospel of Christ. He was found guilty, and amidst a crowd of evil-disposed persons he was led away to the place of execution. The two favorite forms of capital punishment are being sewn up in a wet yak skin and put out in the sun until death ends the torment, or being cast into the depths of a dry well, the top being firmly fastened over the head of the culprit. The latter was chosen for the Sadhu.

Arrived at the place he was stripped of his clothes, and cast into the dark depths of this ghastly charnel-house with such violence that his right arm was injured. Many others had gone down this same well before him never to return, and he alighted on a mass of human bones and rotting flesh. Any death seemed preferable to this. Wherever he laid his hands they met putrid flesh, while the odor almost poisoned him. In the words of his Savior he cried, "Why hast Thou forsaken me?"

Day passed into night, making no change in the darkness of this awful place and bringing no relief by sleep. Without food or even water the hours grew into days, and Sundar felt he could not last much longer. On the third night, just when he had been crying to God in prayer he heard a grating sound overhead. Someone was opening the locked lid of his dismal prison. He heard the key turned and the rattle of the iron covering as it was drawn away. Then a voice reached him from the top of the well, telling him to take hold of the rope that was being let down for his rescue. As the rope reached him he grasped it with all his remaining strength, and was strongly but gently pulled up from the evil place into the fresh air above.

Arrived at the top of the well the lid was drawn over again and locked. When he looked round his deliverer was nowhere to be seen, but the pain in his arm was gone, and the clean air filled him with new life. All that the Sadhu felt able to do was to praise God for his wonderful deliverance, and when morning came he struggled back to the town, where he rested in the serai until he was able to start preaching again. His return to the city and his old work was cause for a great commotion. The news was quickly taken to the Lama that the man they all thought dead was well and preaching again.

The Sadhu was again arrested and brought to the judgment seat of the Lama, and being questioned as to what had happened he told the story of his marvelous escape. The Lama was greatly angered, declaring that someone must have secured the key and gone to his rescue, but when search was made for the key and it was found on his own girdle, he was speechless with amazement and fear. He then ordered Sundar to leave the city and get away as far as possible, lest his powerful God should bring some untold disaster upon himself and his people. Thus was Sundar delivered from a fearful death, and praised God for interposing on his behalf.

Chapter 19
Further Experience In Tibet

"Most gladly will I rather glory in my infirmities that the power of Christ may rest upon me. Therefore I take pleasure . . . in persecutions, in distresses for Christ's sake."-2 Cor. 9:10.

Dr. Fosdick, in his Manhood of the Master, says:-

Jesus made the right attitude toward hostile men not a negative refraining from vengeance, but a positive Saviorhood, that prays for them, blesses them, and sacrificially seeks their good.

This is the attitude of Sadhu Sundar Singh in all his work and life of suffering amongst the peoples of Tibet and other hostile states to whom he carries the Gospel of Christ. In the course of his addresses he sometimes gives illustrations from his own experiences. In speaking on the text, "He that loseth his life shall save it," he told this amazing story. He was one day making a journey across some mountains in Tibet on a bitterly cold day when snow was falling. Both he and a Tibetan companion who was travelling with him were almost frozen to death, and despaired of reaching their journey's end alive. They came to a deep precipice to find a man lying there apparently dead. Sundar suggested they should carry him to a place of safety, but the Tibetan declined, saying it was all they could do to get into safety themselves, and he passed on his way. With difficulty the Sadhu lifted the man on his own back, and began to struggle forward with his heavy load. Soon the exertion brought warmth to him, and communicated itself to the helpless body over his shoulders. He had not gone very far when he overtook his Tibetan companion, who had fallen stone-dead across the path. Eventually Sundar arrived at the village, by which time the half-dead man had recovered consciousness, and they both thanked God for lives snatched from the jaws of death. The Sadhu said he had never known a better practical exposition of the words, "Whosoever will save his life shall lose it, and whosoever will lose his life for My sake shall find it."

On another occasion the Sadhu had been climbing over rough crags when he came to a cave in which he saw a man praying. In order that he should not fall asleep the man had tied his long hair to the roof of the cave, and with closed eyes he strove hour by hour to meditate and pray. Sundar entered the cave and asked the man why he was thus suffering. Like many others this man had spent most of his life in worldly pursuits, but deep down in his mind there was a haunting fear of a dreadful unknown future. This at length drove him to forsake the world, and he had come to this remote spot in the hope of finding satisfaction in prayerful meditation. He explained that no relief had come to his spirit. The Sadhu opened his Testament and read to him such words as, "Come unto Me . . . and I will give you rest."

He proceeded to explain the true way through Jesus Christ. Spellbound the poor fellow listened to the wonderful words, and at last he jumped up crying out, "Now is my soul at rest; make me His disciple, lead me to Him." He begged hard for immediate baptism at the Sadhu's hand, but was persuaded to accompany him to the nearest mission station, where he was left in the care of the missionaries for further instruction.

Sundar tells of another place where his message had met with great hostility and the people were converted into friends by an accident. He was climbing a steep mountain when he slipped and fell, and in his fall a large stone was displaced and rolled over the precipitous cliff on to a place beneath. It happened that just where the stone fell a huge cobra was lying, and was immediately killed. A boy who was herding cattle saw what had happened, and ran to tell the Sadhu, explaining that this very snake had been the cause of some deaths in the village, so that nobody dared to pass along that road. Then he ran to tell the villagers, who were so impressed and so grateful that they welcomed the Sadhu, and here he had the blessed privilege of making known the love of Christ to the ignorant people.

The Feet That Bled

The rough mountain track had torn his feet, and Sundar sat down to bandage the wounds. Another man traversing the same road and seeing what had happened stopped to ask him how he felt. They entered into conversation, and the stranger learnt how that Sundar for his Master's sake day by day walked many weary miles to teach people of Him whose feet had bled on Calvary. The two men held sweet converse together, for he found that his companion, Tashi by name, was an earnest seeker after salvation. But in his quest for truth he was perplexed with many doubts, and these the Sadhu tried to solve. Tashi afterwards said to him, "Looking at your bleeding feet something within me seemed to say there must be some great power behind this happy life of self-denial." And so Tashi urged Snndar to remain with him, and he spent more than a week at his house instructing him and praying with him.

Tashi then sent him on to a Lama who was friendly with him and kindly disposed to Christianity. When he returned he found Tashi full of hope and happiness, for he had found Christ, and now nothing but baptism would satisfy him. All doubts were gone, and Tashi and his family begged that they might now receive baptism. So before leaving, Sundar had the great joy of baptizing Tashi and his whole family-nine persons in all. Being chief secretary to the Lama of the district and a man of importance, Tashi has not been called upon to suffer for his faith, but he is under strict orders not to persuade others to follow his example or in any way to propagate the new faith.

Many a time and oft Sadhu Sundar Singh feels the loneliness

of soul that must come to all whose entire lives are given to spiritual things. Extreme exaltation of spirit accompanied with tremendous expenditure of nervous power must be followed by moments of reaction. Ordinary missionaries and ministers may find respite in change of occupation, but not so the Sadhu. His changes are of place not of work. Day by day his unwearied search for souls continues, and whether in the churches and conventions of Christians or amongst the non-Christian peoples the strain never relaxes. A missionary rightly said of him in Travancore, "He must live very near to God to stand it," and that is the true secret of his being able to continue. Never impatient, never too wearied to meet people who seek him, always gracious, and ready night or day for the tasks that fall to him, he is a living copy of his Master. Sharing his Master's spirit he also shares His loneliness. Speaking of such a time as this he tells of a day when he was unusually tired, hungry, and footsore. Utterly dejected, he was painfully trudging along when he was joined by a man who entered into conversation with him, and so led him out of himself that he forgot his misery in the charming companionship of his new friend. They went on together until they came close to a village, when much to the Sadhu's perturbation he found himself once more alone. He cannot explain it, but his own words are, " I now know that it was an angel of the Lord sent to strengthen and uphold me in my hour of weakness."

Chapter 20
Martyrs Of The Faith

"The blood of the martyrs is the seed of the Church."

"He laid down His life for us; and we ought to lay down our lives for the brethren" (1 John 3:16).

Sadhu Sundar Singh is in the great succession of noble men who have "climbed the steep ascent of heaven," and during his sojourns in Tibet he has come across well-authenticated cases of the martyrdom of godly men who have preceded him in carrying the Gospel message to that dark land. Strangely enough the first of these martyrs came from the State of Patiala where he himself was born. Kartar Singh was a Sikh and the son of a rich zamindar [aristocratic land owner]. All the hopes of the family were centered in this boy, for there were no other sons to carry on the name. Like Sundar he was brought up in the midst of luxury, and preparations for his future were made by giving him the best education possible. Nothing was forgotten that could make his training complete for the fulfillment of his father's ambitions for the boy. But in spite of the utter neglect of religion in his education, there grew up in his mind a desire after spiritual things which his secular training could not satisfy. He heard of Christianity, and little by little got to know and understand its claims, until a deep conviction of its truth laid hold of him. The more he studied it the more he felt it supplied the craving of his own soul, until at last he saw but one path before him- and that the strait and narrow one.

Kartar now took the irrevocable step of declaring himself a Christian, a fact that filled the hearts of his people with dismay.

Many attempts of various kinds were made to win him from persisting in this determination, but finding him not to be tempted by ordinary means his father sent to him the beautiful girl who was his chosen wife. This poor girl came before him in all her tender promise of life, and with tears besought him to desist from taking a step that would mean such terrible loss to her. Looking upon her misery his heart was touched, yet even in this last temptation God gave him strength, and with much tenderness he put the sweet Hindu child from him, declaring that his heart already belonged to Christ his Savior. The broken-hearted girl returned to her future father-in-law's house to tell how useless had been her protests, since Kartar had said all his love had been given to Another.

Not long afterwards Kartar was driven forth homeless from his father's house. To enable him to buy food and clothes he took up the work of a laborer, and, undiscouraged by his hard lot, bent his back to tasks such as his own father's servants would have despised. Very soon, however, Kartar began his mission to the people of his own country, and went preaching among the towns and villages of Patiala, where he trod the thorny and difficult path that was to prepare him for the harder future awaiting him. After preaching in many places in the Punjab, Kartar turned his steps towards the mountains that lay between him and darkest Tibet, and after some weeks of weary journeying over rough country he found himself in the land of his choice.

The Buddhism of Tibet has no place for Christ, whose very name arouses the deepest feelings of hatred and opposition. No record remains that Kartar met with much personal kindness or that his message was accepted, but no thought of going back seems to have occurred to his mind. These people were without Christ and had need of Him, and as Christ had given His life, so Kartar was prepared to sacrifice his life also, that at least his witness should be borne and his love testified to before his persecutors. Although hearts were touched by the sight of his youth and the fervor of his message, there was little courage to take his part, and it was only after his death that the fruit of his labors and testimony came to light.

Kartar saw, as our Savior did before him, that the thorny path could only end in one way. In spite of numerous efforts to drive him out of the country, he continued his preaching in many places for some time, but eventually he was haled before the Lama of Tsingham and charged with unlawfully entering the country with intent to teach a foreign religion. The end he had looked forward to had come, and with undaunted courage he faced the inevitable, trusting to God to give him the necessary grace to witness to his faith to the end. As Sundar afterwards heard, Kartar heard his sentence without a quiver, and with firm step turned away from the judgment seat to walk to the place of execution. On the way he delivered his last message, urging on the crowd the necessity of seeking salvation through Jesus Christ, and one at least of those who heard his words remembered them, and through them found the Savior.

Arrived at the place of execution Kartar was stripped of all his clothes and was sewn up in a wet yak skin, which was then put out in the sun. A cruel mocking crowd stood about to witness his tortures, and as the skin shrank and tightened round him they laughed to hear the bones cracking in the slow process of death. By his side on the ground lay the New Testament that had been his one and only comfort through the hard days that had followed his confession of his Master. Unheeded it lay until on the third day, when Kartar knew the end was drawing on, he asked that his right hand might be set free for a moment. This was done, probably more from curiosity than mercy. Collecting all his strength Kartar wrote his last message on the flyleaf of his Testament. In Persian character:-

Jan Khwaham az Khuda na yake balki sad bazar.
Ta sad hazar bar bamiram brae yar.

Khasrawa dar ishq aukamtarzi Hindu zan mubash,
Ki in brie murda sazad zinda jan i Khwesh ra.

In Urdu character:-

Jan de di di hiii usi ki thi; haqq to yih hai, ki haqq ada na hua.

In English:-

Is this a death-bed where a Christian lies?
Yes, but not his; 'tis death itself there dies.

Translation:-

From God I life besought, not once but a hundred thousand
times,
That to that Friend again as oft I might return it.
That love for Him, Khasrawa, shall not be less than hers-
The faithful Hindu wife,
Who on the burning pyre draws to her heart the loved one,
And lays her life beside him.
The life He gave to me was what I gave to Him;
True is it that though I did all, yet all I could not do.

No cry of anguish escaped the brave lips, but as evening came on Kartar gave thanks aloud to God for comfort in death, and quietly passed away with the words, "Lord Jesus, receive my spirit."

Sadhu Similar Singh found that Kartar's father was still alive, and upon his return to the plains he sought the old man out. Telling him the story of the death of his heroic son and speaking of the great love of Christ that had borne him through, the old man listened with a softened heart, and Sundar had the joy of hearing him say, "I, too, believe in Him."

Amongst the crowd who watched the passing of Kartar Singh was the chief secretary of the Lama of Tsingham. He noticed the little Testament in which this hero of the cross had written his last message, and taking it up he carried it home and commenced to study it. With the memory still fresh in his mind of the words and conduct of a brave man, his heart was open to receive the message the Book had for him, and in reading it there came new light and joy to him. For some time he pondered the wonderful things he now believed, but, as the realization of them more and more filled his soul, he could no longer keep his secret, and one day revealed to his master, the Lama, that he had given his heart to Jesus. The Lama then declared that he also must die. Pitilessly he was judged and sentenced to the same death as Kartar. Lying in the wet yak skin in the sun was not cruel enough to teach the onlookers that this sort of thing if persisted in would add to the bitter punishment, so red-hot skewers were thrust into his body to increase his agonies. As if his tormentors were weary of waiting for the inevitable end, he was then taken out of the skin, a rope was tied round his mutilated body, and he was dragged through the streets of the town, splinters of wood also being driven under the nails of his feet and hands. His body was then thrown on to a dust heap outside the town and he was left for dead.

Having satisfied their lust for revenge his persecutors departed, and for long he lay unconscious. Very gradually the poor fellow came back to life, and little by little strength returned until he was able to crawl away. When he had recovered from his many wounds, great fear came upon the people to see him whom they had left for dead alive and well again, and to this day no one dares to interfere with him. Superstitious dread of a supernatural power they believe him to possess, prevents attempts to take his life, so that when Sadhu Sundar Singh heard from his lips the story of Kartar, he also heard how wondrously God enables this brave man to continue preaching Christ boldly among the people of Tibet.

These and other histories like them Sadhu Sundar Singh has himself gathered during his missionary journeys through darkest Tibet and other regions where the light of the Gospel has scarcely pierced. To the people of these benighted countries his gentle heart turns with infinite longing and pity, and his burning zeal for Christ and desire to make Him known, convince him that there his appointed task lies. He says, "This is the field which God has given me to work in. I have heard His call to serve Him in these hostile provinces. I am not afraid of the risks. I have to win the crown of martyrdom by laying down my life in these parts for Him."

That Sundar Singh may be used of God to bring Gospel light to the people of these dark places is the prayer of those who know, love, and revere him. But none can pray without earnestly pleading with God to spare his wonderful life, that rather by "labors more abundant" than by the supreme sacrifice he may serve his Master and his generation.

Chapter 21
Sundar's Mystism

The study of a character like that of Sadhu Similar Singh cannot fail to be both interesting and instructive, for in a materialistic age he is a man untouched by materialism. Mr. K. J. Saunders, in the Adventures of the Christian Soul, says:-

> Mysticism is the passionate search of the soul in love with God, and the claim that this search has been rewarded . . . The mystic consciousness is marked by simple, clear, and insistent ideas. . . . Possessing God, the mystic desires nothing more. . . . The passionate love aroused in the heart by Christ . . . explains his clear insight into spiritual things, and the tenacity of his pursuit of lofty ideals.

Thus is Sundar Singh a true Christian mystic, and so closely has he studied the life of Christ as it is written in the New Testament, and so constantly has he imitated His example, that naturally he lives in an atmosphere only now and then enjoyed by the ordinary Christian.

His wandering life of poverty in a country like India brings endless opportunities of recognizing his Father's hand in all things, so that often where others would see only the common mercies of daily life the Sadhu praises God for special help in special need. He is familiar with the deepest agony of soul and with the most intense joy. Nights of prayer alternate with long days of toil for his Lord. Close and prayerful study of the New Testament is combined with equally close communion with Christ. A yearning desire to save lost souls that gives him no respite from his labors is balanced by a deep devotion and love for his Savior that fills his heart with peace, and shines in his face. The things of the spiritual life are more real to him than those of the temporal. So near does he live to the great world of spirits that to him there is nothing strange in the ministry of angels. He looks upon it as God's provision for a great need, and when in his own experience some unusual event has come to pass he simply believes that God cares enough for the individual soul to interpose on its behalf. The mysteries of life and death and the great beyond bring no distress or doubt to his mind, and he does not puzzle the minds of his hearers with them. But deep down in his contemplative mind they hold their place, and are a source of infinite satisfaction to him.

The marvelous records of some of the Sadhu's experiences have preceded him in most places he has visited. Matter-of-fact people have been prejudiced by them, and emotional ones have looked for revelations, and even for miracles performed by him. Yet one and all, after seeing and hearing him, have been struck by his sane teaching and well-balanced mind.

His own version of the deliverances he has had falls so naturally from his lips that it sounds like the straightforward simple statement of a second "Acts of the Apostles." In relating these experiences, Sadhu Sundar Singh says that God has stretched forth His hand to save when nothing else could avail. This is the simplest explanation in view of the fact that for so long, and under such signal difficulties and dangers, the Sadhu has worked in the closed lands of Tibet and Nepal.

Incidents such as the following show the spirit in which the Sadhu takes his deliverances. On one occasion he was preaching in a village of Nepal called Khantzi, where considerable opposition was being shown. The villagers seized him, and rolling him up in a blanket, hustled him out of the place, but a stranger passing by took his part and released him. The day following he was again preaching in the same place, and this so angered the villagers that they took him and bound him by his hands and feet to a tree and left him there. Slowly the day wore on, and being faint for want of food he looked longingly at the fruit on the tree just out of reach. In that strained position he at last fell asleep from exhaustion. In the morning he awoke to find to his amazement that his bonds were loosed. He was lying at the foot of the tree and by his side lay some fruit. He then praised God for the suffering he had endured for Christ's sake, ate the fruit with thankfulness of heart, and went on his way filled with fresh courage to preach the word to those who know it not.

On another occasion when he was in a place called Teri some men told him that in a certain village the people were anxious to hear the Gospel, and they gave him instructions as to the way he should take. Following the directions he wandered on for a long time through marshy jungle country, but without seeing any signs of a village. The undergrowth grew thicker, and presently he discovered he was lost in a jungle from which there seemed no escape. Arrived at a stream he thought that by crossing it he might find a way out, but on stepping into the water he found the current so strong that any attempt to cross it would endanger his life. Evening was closing in, and in a dejected frame of mind he sat down by the stream to consider what next to do. Listening to the weird sounds of the jungle, and watching the increasing darkness, his mind became full of apprehension, for soon the wild animals would steal from their haunts in search of food, and his life would be safe no longer.

He prayed earnestly to God, and then looking across the river in the gathering gloom he caught sight of a man, and the words reached his cars, "I am coming to your help." Then he saw the man plunge into the stream and swim across, and taking the Sadhu on his back he swam to the other shore with him. Arrived on the bank he saw a fire at which he began to dry his wet clothes, but even as he did so the stranger disappeared, and the Sadhu was left to meditate on the wonderful ways of Providence in thus sending help to him in this unaccountable way.

Yet one more instance is worth relating. The Sadhu had been preaching at a place called Kamyan where much bitter enmity had been exhibited. The whole day had passed without his being able to get any food, so, hungry and weary, he found himself in a desert place without shelter for the fast-closing-in night. Very weak and miserable he lay down under a tree and soon fell asleep. About midnight it appeared to him that someone touched him and bade him arise and eat, and upon looking up he beheld two men with food and water standing over him. Imagining that some villagers had had pity on his condition he gratefully partook of the refreshments thus offered to him. When his hunger was satisfied he turned to converse with the men who had brought the food, but there was not a soul to be seen anywhere. How they had disappeared he could not tell, but again he blessed God for His kindly provision for him in time of need.

Doubtless such instances could be multiplied, for in a life like that of Sadhu Sundar Singh there are frequent manifestations of the good hand of God. Without attempting any explanation the Sadhu accepts his deliverances with a thankful mind as coming from God. He simply says, "I know the Lord has stretched forth His own hand to save me "; and whether such deliverances are wrought by human agency or otherwise, he is surely right in ascribing them to the care of a loving heavenly Father.

Chapter 22
The Sadhu's Love For The Cross

"I am crucified with Christ: . . . who loved me, and gave Himself for me" (Gal. 2:20).

"But God forbid that I should glory, save in the cross of the Lord Jesus Christ, by whom the world is crucified unto me, and I unto the world" (Gal. 6:14).

The great theme of all Sadhu Sundar Singh's preaching is Christ. The cross of Christ is the central figure to which he draws all men, for there he himself found peace, and so can speak with authority of the power of that cross to save others. The most frequent words on his lips are words taken from his own experience, "I can say with confidence that the cross will bear those who bear the cross, until that cross shall lift them into the presence of the Savior."

As a Muhammadan said lately to a missionary who had been relating to him the story of the cross, "If you present that story to India as you have to me, India will accept it." Thus has the Sadhu found the heart of India, and he presents to it the one and only satisfaction for its soul hunger-Jesus and His Cross. He presents it in the New Testament way, and his life of utter self-abnegation and sacrifice enforces his teaching, while his own intense personal joy in the Savior commends it as nothing else could. The cross implies suffering, and to be like his Lord is the one desire of the Sadhu. He wrote in an autograph book:-

So great the joy I have in Light
That every sorrow brings delight.

A missionary in Japan asked the Sadhu whether he still wandered about India hungry and homeless as he had done in the beginning of his Christian ministry, and was struck by the reply: "No, now in India they know me, and if I go to a town they have thousands of people to hear me in a big hall. This is not the way of the Cross; for that I must go to Tibet."

While surrounded by almost adoring crowds in Trivandram, his one grief was that things were so comfortable that he was not suffering for his Master enough. Perhaps later, when he was rushed from place to place for countless meetings in the heat of our tropical summer-a heat he had not experienced before, always having from a child spent the hot season on the hills- and having to travel by boat, bullock cart, or train at night, and to start his work again upon arrival, he may have felt differently. In speaking of it to his friends he simply said, "It is the will of God."

When he was plunged into the misery of an eastern prison at Horn to find himself herded with all sorts of evil characters, he wrote in the fly-leaf of his New Testament these words :-

Nepal, June 7, 1914. "'Christ's presence has turned my prison into a blessed heaven; what then will it do in heaven hereafter?"

So, like his predecessors Paul and Silas of old, his prison was his meeting-place with Christ, and to be in hell with Christ would be better to him than to be in heaven without Him.

So sure is the Sadhu of Christ's continual presence with him that he expressed no surprise when the following event took place in his life. When travelling through a wild part of Tibet and unable to enter the village because of the hostility of the people the Sadhu took refuge in a cave. He had not been there long when he saw a number of the village people approaching him with sticks and stones, and feeling that his end was near he commended his soul to

God in prayer. Within a few yards of him the men suddenly stood still, and falling back some paces they began to whisper together. Then again they came forward and said to the Sadhu, "Who is the other man with you in bright garments, and many more who surround you?" He replied that there was no man with him, but with awe the men insisted that they saw a host of bright ones standing all round the cave. Then the men besought the Sadhu to accompany them to their homes, and going with them he spoke of Christ so that they feared and believed his words. He then knew that God had sent His angels to protect him in danger and to open the way for him to preach to these men. A few years ago the Sadhu wrote:-

I thank God that He has chosen unworthy me in the days of my youth that I may spend the days of my strength in His service. Even before baptism my prayer to God was that He should show me His ways, and so He, who is the Way, the Truth, and the Life, did show Himself to me, and called me to serve Him as a sadhu and to preach His holy Name. Now although I have suffered hunger, thirst, cold, heat, imprisonment, maledictions, infirmities, persecutions, and innumerable evils, yet I thank and bless His holy Name that through His grace my heart is ever full of joy. From my ten years' experience I can unhesitatingly say that the Cross bears those who bear the Cross.

Today the Sadhu bears the same testimony to the writer, adding that he hopes God will spare him yet for some years, that the fullness of manhood's strength may all be given to Him in the precious work of preaching, or in suffering, wheresoever his Lord may send him.

Chapter 23
Sadhu Sundau Singh And The Sanyasi Mission

It was surely a wonderful provision of God when He called Sundar Singh to be a Christian Sadhu. Amongst Christians his saffron robe gives him a position the best possible for the acceptance of the message he brings. Granted the same man and message he would assuredly under any circumstances have won the heart of the Indian Christian Church, but being a true Sadhu in appearance as well as in spirit has added enormously to his influence and power.

Perhaps nothing has proved more wonderful to Christians everywhere than the humility and simplicity of the Sadhu's spirit, and no one is more filled with wonder than himself when crowds linger about him just to look at his face.

But the most remarkable results of his being a Sadhu are apparent in his life and work amongst non-Christians. This he looks upon as his sworn task. Naturally his sadhu's robes gain him 'an entrance to places and to people as nothing else could,, Often in the course of his pilgrimages from place to place he comes across unusual types of Indian sadhus, and it has been his privilege to discover to the world a marvelous movement towards Christianity amongst the most deeply religious men of India.

The Rev. J. J. Johnson, of the Church Missionary Society, who died in 1918, was one of the finest Sanskrit scholars in India. During the latter part of his life, he was set apart by his Society for a work he was magnificently fitted for amongst the pandits and learned classes throughout India. The story of this work is a romance waiting to be written. On his last visit to the south he told us that he believed there were great numbers of the highest castes of India waiting to become Christians, a statement made after years of intimate relationship with the leaders of religious thought in India.

But it was reserved for Sundar Singh to lift the veil and prove the truth of this astonishing statement, and this is how it came about. Towards the end of 1912 the Sadhu went to Sarnath (the scene of Buddha's first preaching), and there he met with some men dressed as sanyasis. Entering into conversation with them he found they were Christians, and belonged to a secret organization numbering some 24,000 members, who are scattered all over India. These are divided into two classes called Shishyas and Swamis, or Companions and Heralds. The Companions are ordinary members who fulfill all the usual work of life. The Heralds number about 700, are dressed like Sanyasis, and are the unpaid preachers who conduct services among the Companions wherever they meet them.

These secret believers observe baptism and the Lord's Supper. Bands of them are found all over India, and in most distant and unexpected places. It was due to the kindness and care of some of these good people that Sundar was on one occasion nursed back to life after imprisonment and persecution in Nepal. He says that these believers are wont to assemble at fixed and very early hours in "Houses of Prayer" outwardly resembling Hindu temples, but which contain no images or pictures. The Bible is read and expounded and Christian papers are circulated. Eastern methods are sedulously followed, such as complete prostration of the body in prayer. The belief is held that if men prayed in perfect faith they would have constant visions of the Master Himself.

Belonging to this secret Christian Brotherhood are various sadhus and hermits of recognized holiness, and a large number of the members are educated and wealthy men of the upper classes, who freely subscribe towards the maintenance of the organization. The Sadhu has often been present at their services, and has several times been mistaken for one of themselves. He has very earnestly begged that they would openly confess Christ, and they promise that when the right moment comes they will do so.

On one occasion while the Sadhu was preaching on the banks of the Ganges his audience told him that while they liked him as a sanyasi they did not like his message, and they requested him to visit a great Hindu preacher who lived close by and who was attracting large crowds. For three days he could not get near him for the crowd. One day, however, he was able to meet him alone, and then the Sadhu learnt that he was a Christian. The Hindu preacher embraced him and said, "Brother, we are doing the same work." Surprised at this, Sundar said he had never heard him preaching Christ. To which he replied, "Is there any foolish farmer who will sow without preparing the ground? I first try to awaken in my hearers a sense of values, and when a hunger and thirst for righteousness is created I place Christ before them. On the banks of this ancient river I have baptized twelve educated Hindus during the past year." He then showed him the Bible he always carried about with him.

In one of the holy cities of India some of these secret believers took the Sadhu to an old temple, where they showed him an ancient Sanskrit manuscript containing an account of Pandit Viswa Mitra, one of the three Wise Men who, after seeing the Divine Child, came back to India but returned at a later date to Palestine when Christ had entered on His public ministry. They claim that he was the one of whom the disciples complained to the Master that they found him performing miracles and forbade him "because he walketh not with us." This parchment also gives in modern Sanskrit a history of the Brotherhood during later days.

The Sanyasi Mission does not appear to have flourished much until the days of Carey, when some Christian Sanyasis heard the Gospel from his lips and were fired with fresh enthusiasm. From that time the mission prosecuted its work with quickened faith and its numbers began to increase.

In one of the large northern cities the Sadhu was introduced to a famous Hindu preacher who was considered a profound scholar in the Vedas. He heard him lecture on the Hindu Scriptures, and towards the end the lecturer said, "The Vedas reveal to us the need of redemption from sin, but where is the redeemer? The 'Prajapathi,' [a group Hindu deity] of whom the Vedas speak, is Christ who has given His life as a ransom for sinners." When questioned afterwards by Hindus the lecturer said, "It is I who believe in the Vedas and not you, because I believe in Him whom the Vedas reveal, that is Christ."

In speaking of this the Sadhu declared that the great need of our age is that the Church should have a broad vision; that the Christian should transcend the limitations of sect and creed, and be prepared to recognize the Spirit of God in whatever form He may be made manifest. He added that he fully believed the Sanyasi Mission is being blessed of God, and although it has taken a form we are not accustomed to, it is given to its leaders to do great things for India.

Yishu Nasri Nath ki Jai- "Victory to Jesus Lord of Nazareth"- is the password of this secret Brotherhood of Christians in India.

Chapter 24
Sadhu Sundar Singh And The Maharishi Of Kailash

Some time ago a North Indian newspaper published the following:-

> Our worldless, selfless, and godly brother Sundar Singh has discovered the Christian hermit the Maharishi at Kailash, who has for years been on the snowy Himalayas praying and interceding for the world. . . . You have revealed to the world the secret of one of the members of our mission the Maharishi at Kailash.

During his pilgrimage in Western Tibet the Sadhu was constantly searching for those holy men who retire to the snowy peaks and caves of these distant mountains, there to spend their last days in contemplation. Far from the dwellings of men in the silence of the eternal snows stretches the Kailash range of the Himalayas. The mighty Indus has its source in this range, and its great tributary, the Sutlej, also takes its rise there. The Sutlej flows through the country of Sundar Singh's birth, and at one point where the bed of the stream is 8,494 feet above the level of the sea, the rocky gorge presents a scene of awful sublimity, and is one of the natural wonders of the world.

On the summit of one of the mountains of the Kailash Range is a deserted Buddhist temple now rarely visited by man. A few miles from this temple dwells the great saint known as the Maharishi of Kailash, in a cave some 13,000 feet above sea level. All this region is the Olympus of India, the seat of Hindu holy myths, and it is associated in Hindu sacred books with the names of great and devout souls of all times. In one cave the Sadhu found the skeleton of some nameless holy man who had died while meditating there.

The scenery all around is grand and impressive, and amidst the everlasting snows, springs of boiling water bubble up from out the frozen ground. Some three days' journey from this place is the famous Lake Manasarowar, an exquisitely beautiful and holy place. On the Lake float many fine swans, and upon the overhanging cliffs, in sweet picturesqueness, are perched ancient Buddhist temples and monasteries. The Sadhu describes this as one of the loveliest places he has ever seen, but he also adds that here too are found the most cruel of nomadic tribes, who slay for the pure love of it, and thus convert the place into a terror to the harmless pilgrims travelling through it.

In the summer of 1912 he travelled through these regions alone and on foot, often refreshed by the beautiful scenes through which he passed, but more often fatigued to the last degree in his difficult and fruitless search for the holy men he hoped to meet there. He will never forget the day when, struck with snow-blindness and almost wearied to death, he staggered drearily on over snowy and stony crags not knowing whither he went. Suddenly he lost his balance and fell. Recovering from the fall he awoke to one of the greatest experiences of his life, for he opened his eyes to find himself lying outside a huge cave, in the shelter of which sat the Maharishi of Kailash in deep meditation.

The sight that met his eyes was so appalling that Sundar closed them and almost fainted. Little by little he ventured to make an inspection of the object before him, and then discovered that he was looking at a living human being, but so old and clothed with long hair as to appear at first glance like an animal. Sundar realized that thus unexpectedly he had succeeded in his search after a holy man, and as soon as he could command his voice, he spoke to the aged saint. Recalled from his meditation, the saint opened his eyes and, casting a piercing glance upon the Sadhu, amazed him by saying, "Let us kneel and pray." Then followed a most earnest Christian prayer ending in the name of Jesus. This over, the Maharishi unrolled a ponderous copy of the Gospels in Greek, and read some verses from Matthew, chapter 5. The Sadhu heard from his own lips the account of his wonderful life. He claimed to be of very great age. The roll from which he had read he explained had come down to him from Francis Xavier, and the Sadhu noticed that it was all written in Greek Uncials, and may therefore prove to be of value to scholars should it come into their possession. The Saint said he was born in Alexandria of a Muhammadan family, and was brought up to be a zealous follower of the prophet. At the age of thirty he renounced the world and entered a monastery in order to give himself up entirely to religion. But the more he read the Qur'an and prayed, the more unhappy he became. During these days of spiritual distress he heard of a Christian saint who had gone over from India to preach in Alexandria, and from him he heard words of life that filled his hopeless soul with joy. He now left the monastery to accompany his teacher in his missionary journeys. After some time spent thus, permission was given him to go on his own account to preach the Gospel wherever God sent him. The Saint then started out on an evangelistic campaign that continued a very long time.

At last, wearied with his strenuous labors, the Saint resolved to spend the remainder of his days in the secluded spot where Sundar found him. During the years spent in this place the Saint has learnt much about the products of the mountains and jungles around him, by means of which he has been able to subsist to this day. When the Sadhu first met him he was chilled to the bone by the bitter cold. The Saint gave him the leaves of a certain plant to eat, which having eaten he immediately felt a comfortable glow steal over his body.

The Sadhu had long conversations with him about holy things, and heard many strange things from his lips. Some of the excellent illustrations Sundar uses in his sermons were given him by this aged Saint. The Maharishi belongs to the Sanyasi Mission. His astonishing visions, as related to the Sadhu, would, if written down, read like another Book of Revelation, so strange and incomprehensible are they. The Sadhu himself warns readers and hearers of these visions that common interpretations can never disclose their meaning, since the Saint has to clothe his ideals in language that cannot be taken literally. Sundar Singh has visited the Maharishi three times, and hopes to see him again at some future time.

Sundar reading the New Testament

Chapter 25
Sadhu Sundar Singh In South India

"I speak . . . those things which I have heard of Him ... as My Father hath taught me, I speak these things" (John 8:26, 28).

"Obey I beseech thee the voice of the Lord, which I speak unto thee; so shall . . . thy soul live" (Jer. 38:20).

Without any idea of the protracted tour in front of him, the Sadhu came down to Madras at the beginning of 1918, intending to visit a few places before starting for Tibet. But his fame had preceded him, and invitations poured in upon him from all over South India. An offer voluntarily made by a gentleman in Madras to act as interpreter for a few weeks caused him to alter his plans, and to accept a program which eventually included Travancore and Ceylon.

Every day fresh entreaties reached him from all directions, and out of them grew that great evangelistic tour not only through the South and Ceylon, but also Burma, the Federated Malay States, China, and Japan.

The large Christian community of South India provided an immense sphere for his operations, and, regardless of distinction of caste or creed, thousands flocked to his meetings everywhere. His -work was varied and strenuous. Often the day's work began so early and continued so late that he had scarcely time for meals, and no leisure even for the study of his New Testament. In places where he spent many days the people rested after his departure as a man does after a good meal; but in no place did people imagine that the Sadhu needed rest.

Long days of engagements were succeeded by a wearisome night's journey by boat, bullock cart, or train. The new day's work began upon arrival and continued until departure. Public meetings were usually held morning and evening, and for hours between the Sadhu sat receiving visitors and holding interviews, when he gave advice, solved the religious problems that were presented to him, and answered enquirers as far as he was able. The number present on such occasions varied from a single person to a hundred or more. The value of these meetings was testified to by the witness of those who attended them, as also by the fact that the longer the Sadhu stayed in a place the greater were the numbers who sought to see him.

In one place where great numbers sought him for spiritual guidance a student in the hostel where he stayed made it his happy duty to watch over him by admitting the visitors. The young man kept the key of the Sadhu's door, and as the time for devotions or meals came round some small measure of privacy and rest was assured.

In large centers where there were colleges and high schools, these were visited between morning and evening meetings, and addresses were given to the students. The acceptance of invitations to private houses to meet parties of Christians, involved extra work at the close of arduous days. The barrier of language was a difficulty in the south, where so many Dravidian tongues are spoken. Wherever possible interviews were conducted in English, but at many of these, as well as in public, the Sadhu was often obliged to speak by interpretation, and that not always of the best. To one so ardent in temperament, so full of his message, so anxious for souls, this language difficulty was a very real one, but to see him at these times no one would surmise his feelings.

The Sadhu seeks for no disciples to follow his example. He rightly holds that a man must have a distinct call of God to embark on such a life. His advice to all is sane, wise, suited to the people to whom it is given. His devout mother's, example in bringing him up to reverence religion is a constant parable of life in his talks to women. He often says, "If a non-Christian mother can do so much for her son, how much more can you Christian mothers do for your sons?" Deeply loving the New Testament himself, he speaks of Christians loving it more than he, since they have never torn and burnt it as he once did, but have been trained to honor and love it. How conscience-stricken many of his hearers are when they hear him say this, he does not know!

It has been no uncommon thing during the Sadhu's stay in South India for Hindus to seek him in the silent hours of the night, when he will "spend and be spent" in their service while others sleep. Growing demands were made on his time and strength, by the numbers of letters he received from people in places he had visited, and the requests for his prayers were legion.

Christians by thousands, who have seen Sadhu Sundar Singh, behold in him what it is possible for God to make of it man who submits himself soul and body to his Savior, and so long as he is visible, people never grow weary of looking at him. They have received him and his message with great joy wherever he has been, the only regret being that he could not stay longer to consolidate his work. How deep) and far-reaching the results of his work are only God knows, but that his coming was timely and that God sent him, none can for a moment doubt. He places before men the true ideal of a godly life of self-surrender to Christ, and of self-abnegation in His service.

Chapter 26
Sadhu Sundar Singh At A Great Christian Convention

THE CALL. "Oh, Young Men, awake and see how many souls are daily perishing around you. Is it not your duty to save them? Be brave soldiers of Christ; Go forward in full amour; Crush Satan's work and victory be yours.

"Glory to God. He has given you a precious opportunity to be saved and to save others. If you are careless now, you will never get another chance. Whatever you have got to do, do it now. For you will never pass through the field of battle again. The day is fast approaching when you will see the martyrs in their glory, who gave their health, wealth and life to win souls for Christ. They have done much. What have you done? Oh! may we not blush on that day."-Sundar Singh.

This clarion call resounded all through South India, stirring hearts everywhere; but perhaps nowhere was it so clear, so insistent, as at the conventions of Christians in Travancore and Ceylon. Where Christians are numerous, annual conventions for the deepening of spiritual life have of late years, become very popular. Like the Keswick Convention, meetings are held for a week with settled programs and preachers, and are attended by increasing numbers as time goes on. Several of the conventions have been blessed by the presence of the Sadhu, the largest in point of numbers being in Travancore.

The historic Syrian Church of Malabar proudly dates back to the days when it is believed that St. Thomas landed on these shores and laid the foundations of Christianity in India. This ancient Church is divided into three sections, the Roman, the Jacobite and the Mar Thoma Syrian.

About the middle of February, 1918, the Sadhu attended the Jacobite Syrian Convention in North Travancore, when some 20,000 people came together, and he spent a happy and useful time amongst them. From there at the end of the month he went on to the Mar Thoma Syrian Convention, also in North Travancore.

This latter was a romantic and remarkable experience not soon to be forgotten. A hundred miles north of Trivandram is the widest and most beautiful river of Travancore. In the dry season the river flows only in the deepest parts of its bed. A big bend in the river leaves a very large sandy island upon which each year an immense booth is erected to accommodate 25,000 people. For a week meetings are carried on during the greater part of each day. Every day long before dawn a man with a stentorian voice passed round the encampment crying, "Praise be to God! Praise to the Son of God!" Very soon after the sound of prayer rose all around. These prayers were chanted to ancient Syrian tunes, the weird sound rising in gradual crescendo; and thus was the blessing of God invoked before the meetings each day. The Sadhu drew greater crowds than usual, so that before the end of the week the booth had to be enlarged, and at the final meeting no fewer than 32,000 people gathered to hear his last message.

The wonder of that daily scene is almost beyond description. A rough platform about eighteen inches high had been placed about a third of the way from the back of the booth, and on one end stood two chairs occupied by the two Bishops of the Mar Thoma Syrian Church, who appeared daily in resplendent robes of red or purple satin with gold belts and quaint head-dresses. On the platform below, sitting tailor fashion, were the clergy of the Church, and in front of them in the same lowly style sat the Sadhu.

The vast crowds were seated on the sand, the women all in white on the left, and the men in front and at the right. Away over the sea of heads one caught glimpses of the shining river, with its strange craft plying up and down. A more devout crowd it is not possible to imagine Every day the early part of the meetings was given to prayer. Subjects were given for silent prayer from time to time by the presiding Bishop, when every head was bowed, and the almost inaudible murmur of prayer gradually increased until a sound like the surging sea lolling in full tide rose all around-a most impressive experience!

The fearful heat was only equaled by the intense silence that prevailed as the Sadhu rose to speak. Often, in his northern country he had heard of the great number of Christians in Travancore, and thousands had gathered in our own mission to hear him. But here for the first time he realized, as he looked at this mighty crowd how great the number was; and his heart was filled with wonder as to why the Gospel had been so long in reaching the millions of greater India.

In brave stern words he reminded this multitude that through the ages God had made the Syrian Church the repository of His truth, but that failure on their part to hand on the Gospel to their own countrymen had forced God to call men from America and England to do the work they had left undone. Then, alluding to the great reform movement in this ancient Church, he earnestly and tenderly besought them to rise to the call-unheard for so long-and send the light to the millions who are still dying in darkness.*

This same appeal has been made in other places since then, and the hearts of people have been stirred to this great issue as never before. The Sadhu clearly sees the duty and privilege God is offering to the Indian Church to enter into His purposes, and claim for Him the myriads of this ancient land. By his own example, as well as by his words, he urges India's sons to take up their cross at all costs, and follow Christ to final victory.

* The Syrian Church in Travancore has been alive to this great need for some years, and is continually increasing the number of missionaries it has begun to send to different parts of India.

Chapter 27
Ceylon

"Thou shalt be His witness . . . of what thou hast seen and heard." -- Acts 20:15

In May, 1918, the Sadhu had almost completed a long and arduous tour through South India. Before passing west and north again he left the great continent of his birth, and crossing to Colombo spent six weeks in Ceylon. During those crowded weeks the enthusiasm of the south was repeated in every place he visited, and increasingly as the days went by. Probably for the first time in Ceylon missionaries, ministers, and laymen of all denominations joined together for a campaign that should cover most of the important towns of the Island; and their harmonious co-operation not only made things run smoothly for the Sadhu, but largely contributed to the very real success of his work. Everything was done to ensure his visiting as many places as possible, and local papers in Colombo, Kandy, and Jaffna reported his progress as he went along.

Mr. Wilson, the convener of the committee that arranged his program, wrote:-

His (the Sadhu's) meetings were always attended by enormous crowds. People began to come in from 3 o'clock when the meetings were announced to begin at 6 p.m.Catholics and Hindus came in great numbers, and people from as far as forty miles off came to Colombo to attend the meetings. At no place could a hall be got large enough to hold the crowds that thronged to hear him day after day. Drawing-room meetings were arranged in many places. Probably no Christian evangelical effort so greatly stirred the people as this mission of an Indian convert garbed as a sanyasi. There was no way of translating the addresses into Sinhalese. An attempt was made, but proving unsatisfactory the idea was abandoned.

A Hindu gentleman well acquainted with the recent revival literature of Hinduism was desirous of putting into the question-box a question relating to prayer. By a happy coincidence that night the Sadhu spoke on prayer. The man listened very attentively, and at the end he said, "He is really a spiritual guru (teacher) and I hope to get light from him."

In Jaffna, a large city on the north of the Island, a real spiritual work was done. In writing of the Sadhu the Rev. G. G. Brown, M.A., a missionary in Jaffna, said of the Sadhu:-

He has a deep and unique religious experience, yet it is with great hesitancy that he speaks about it, and he never gives the impression that his should be the normal experience, or that others should follow his manner of living. His hold on the people is real, and I have never seen large meetings at Jaffna at which the attention was so marked. Part of his charm and power lies in the fact that he represents a purely Indian type of life and thought, and in him we have an expression of Christian ideals in a purely Indian setting.

Invitations were scattered broadcast amongst nonChristians which were well responded to by Buddhists, Muhammadans, and Hindus, and they were assured that if they came "with an open mind they should not return without gain." In several places, especially in Jaffna, after the Sadhu's departure, articles appeared in the local papers earnestly urging a practical issue, and inviting college and school teachers as well as ministers to follow up the work while hearts were likely to be responsive to the message of life.

The Sadhu often addressed as many as three meetings a day, as well as conducting interviews, and he suffered so much from the moist heat that in writing to a friend in the north he likened himself to a lump of salt in solution, adding, he was "willing to melt like salt if only the south might be salted."

The Sadhu's tour, both through Ceylon and South India, was a remarkable experience. In Colombo every day hundreds could not get near the doors of his meetings, and from dawn to late at night great numbers sought him out for spiritual guidance, so that all the time his life was lived amongst crowds. Newspapers wrote about him, and his name became a household word in thousands of Christian homes. But multitudes and popularity count for nothing to the Sadhu beyond the fact that they provide for him opportunities to preach Christ and reach the souls of men. At what cost this great work has been done only the Sadhu himself knows. His calm dignity amongst the enormous crowds that surrounded him and invaded his privacy at all hours, gave no hint of his innermost shrinking from such great publicity.

One great safeguard to the Sadhu in the enormous temptations such experiences bring, is his absolute simplicity, that simplicity which Fenelon describes as "an uprightness of soul which has ceased to dwell upon itself or its actions," where Christ is all and selfless than the dust.

On his return to Colombo after touring the Island he held a series of meetings, when his addresses were translated from Urdu into English by Canon Goldsmith, who went over from Madras for the purpose.

In many parts of Ceylon the Sadhu was much impressed by the apparent wealth of the people and their love of display. He spoke frequently and clearly everywhere with regard to the hindrance these things are to a true and simple Christian life, and he urged that humbler Christians should not be hindered in their higher life, since they could only reluctantly enter churches where such exhibitions were indulged in.

He found here as in the South that the spirit of caste amongst Christians seriously militated against spiritual progress, and he was as unsparing in his condemnation as he was tender in his pleading that this great stumblingblock should be removed.

In his own inimitable Way Sadhu Sundar Singh used a striking simile when he compared India to a giant, the snowy Himalayas being the head, and South India the feet. Putting his finger on the weak spot in the armor of Southern Christianity he said, "It is with the feet of South Indian Christians that Christianity can walk in India. But alas! although the feet are there, apparently strong and well-shaped they cannot walk. What is, wrong? As in the case of a man I saw in Cochin, there is elephantiasis in the feet, and this elephantiasis is the spirit of caste."

Who can speak with greater authority on this subject than Sadhu Sundar Singh himself? Like Paul, who declared himself "a Hebrew of the Hebrews, "so may the Sadhu claim to be "a Sikh of the Sikhs" -one of the proudest names in India; but instead his life testifies to the words, "God forbid that I should glory, save in the cross of Jesus Christ, by whom the world is crucified unto me and I unto the world."

In passing through Ceylon and India the Sadhu has made his appeal. Well might he say, "Be ye followers of me" in this great matter. When will the great Christian Church accept and abide by his teaching and example, and casting off the chains of centuries enter into that "fullness of life" of which the Sadhu so constantly spoke, and which he himself enjoys? Thus, and thus only, shall she enter into that abundant and glorious service that shall claim India for her Lord.

The visit of Sadhu Sundar Singh to the Churches of South India and Ceylon is over. His work is done, and he has passed to other lands and other communities. The hearts of thousands have been touched by his message and his personality, and though eminently practical he has stirred deep emotions in every place he has been to. Probably no single man has attracted so much attention and devotion in all the history of the Christian Church in India.

During his visit people constantly besought him to pray for them; to visit and pray with sick friends and to bless little children; and even to touch his robe brought comfort to many. As the Sadhu continued his journey through the South, these requests and this treatment became so general, and reports of his having healed the sick by his touch or through prayer so persistent, that he was obliged to decline requests to visit the homes of people, lest super-stitious beliefs should cause them to look upon him as a worker of miracles. When asked to bless people his reply invariably was, "How can these hands bless anyone-these hands that tore up God's Word and burnt it in the fire?"

Not by such means did Sundar Singh strive to bring men to the feet of his Master 1 But by forceful message and by a living exam-ple he showed men how to tread the same path, and with persua-sive tenderness he sought to lead them to the Savior. Is Sundar Singh to pass leaving only a burning message and precious memory?

Greater than the blessing of his hands, greater than his person-ality, is the deep desire of his heart that the Christians of India and Ceylon may accept his ministry, put it into practice, live by it, and with him become true and devoted followers of Jesus Christ.

Let us arise, and, "His grace abiding," follow Sadhu Sundar Singh even as he follows Christ.

Chapter 28
"Unto The Uttermost Parts Of The Earth"

"I live by the faith of the Son of God."- Galatians 2:20.

Returning in July to India the Sadhu completed his work in the South, turning west to Bombay for a conference and then north to Calcutta, where soon after his arrival he fell ill of influenza which was raging there at the time. In writing of this afterwards he said, "In sickness God has given me the rest and time for prayer I could not get in the South." Upon his recovery he went to spend a few days at Bolpur with the great Eastern Mystic, Sir Rabindranath Tagore, returning to Calcutta to obey a call to visit Burma and the Straits Settlements. The continuous messages of affection he kept receiving from Ceylon during these and succeeding days brought him a great deal of happiness.

On his way over the seas to Burma he wrote, "I have much time for prayer and am reading many new pages in the book of nature," and all who know him will understand how his store of illustrations would be enriched from that source in a way entirely his own. Arrived at Rangoon he had the assistance of translators and still did most of his work in Urdu, but even at that time he was hoping soon to be able to speak in English and so avoid the double and even treble translations that weakened his messages and were such a source of trouble to him. Private moments were given to the study of English, and wherever possible he practiced speaking it.

Here and in other cities he was followed by an Arya Samaj preacher who strove to undo his work by pouring forth violent invectives against Christianity, but people were not attracted to hear

him, and he eventually gave up in disgust. At one of his meetings
Sundar Singh invited the people to contribute to the funds of the
Indian National Missionary Society, when a thank-offering of Rs.
500 was immediately raised for that purpose.

As in South India and Ceylon, so here a crowded program
awaited him. The visit of Bishop Lefroy to Rangoon earlier on had
prepared the way for a good reception. The Bishop of Rangoon
took the chair at one of his meetings, when numerous thank-
offerings for his work were made to God. These provided the Sadhu with the necessaries of life, and met his travelling expenses in
Burma and to China and Japan.

All through his life as a Sadhu, Sundar Singh has taken God at
His word, "Take no thought for your life, what ye shall eat . . . put
on," and God has amply rewarded his faith. To pass alone from
India through Burma, Mandalay, Perak, Singapore, Penang, and
away to China and Japan, with their varying climates, peoples, and
languages, without money and with only a foreign language as his
medium of communication with strange races, staggers the imagi-
nation of ordinary people. But the same faith that in earlier years
made him turn his back upon his home, and took him while yet a
boy to the wilds of inhospitable Tibet, enabled him to go at God's
call to these distant places without a moment's hesitation or doubt,
and that at a time when, as Mr. K. T. Paul says, "the whole of the
Indian Church was at his feet and he could have had anything he
wanted." He is a man so gladly obedient to his God that he steps
out into an utterly unknown future unprovided for, and lo! trains
stand ready for him, ships ride at anchor awaiting him, and men of
different nationalities, colors, and languages hold out helping
hands everywhere. Surely this is living " by the faith of the Son of
God"!

In the cosmopolitan cities of Rangoon, Singapore, and Penang
the large audiences were perhaps as mixed in race, status, and language as anywhere in the world. Here the Sadhu came in contact
with Chinese, Japanese, Malays, Europeans, and various Indian
peoples, and his addresses were usually translated by two inter-
preters. Urdu, Burmese, Bengali, Tamil, Telugu, Chinese, and

English were the means of communication, while business men of different races, army men, clerics, and Government officials took the chair or shared the same platform with him.

For lack of Christian newspapers to report his work, and since he so rarely of his own accord speaks about it, information regarding his tour has been difficult to obtain, but letters from friends who have met or entertained him give glimpses of interest. When the Sadhu went up to Maymyo he was delighted with the fine scenery and cool climate. It was in this beautiful spot that he met some Punjabis, his own countrymen, who, though non-Christians, insisted on his taking a meal with them, and much to his joy invited him to partake from the same dish with . them. A missionary writing from there said:-

Above all his gifts stands out the soul of the man, a soul that has gripped to itself the message it imparts to others. In every city he visited he has left a trail of light behind him.

From Ipoh in Perak came the pathetic message:-

He has taught us to pray, for our prayers are quite different now. My nephew, the son of a non-Christian, has always said he would never become a Christian, but would remain in the faith of his ancestors and perform his father's funeral rites. The Sadhu stayed in our house, and so cleared the young man's doubts that he now wishes to be baptized.

A leading medical man in Singapore sends a brief message:-

His tour through the Malay States, extending over a month, was a continued Pentecost:

While a Straits paper adds:-

His passionate advocacy of the Christian faith won the hearts of his numerous hearers.

At Bassein he was very happy to find that some leading Hindus and Muhammadans were taking an active part in arranging for the meetings, and in Penang another unexpected happiness awaited him. He spoke in the Empire Theatre, the address being summarized in Tamil, Malay, and Chinese. A meeting for Sikhs in Hindustani was held in St. George's Chapel, when he preached to a full house. At the close of the meeting a Sikh gentleman arose and invited the Sadhu to go and speak in the Sikh Temple. At Penang also the Chief of the Police took the chair at one of his meetings, and gave a half-holiday to the police staff in order to give them the opportunity of attending.

It was little wonder that fear was expressed in certain quarters that so much success might wean him from the simple sadhu life. But no one was more alive to the insidious temptations of the moment than the Sadhu himself, and his constant prayer was that he might be kept humble and faithful to the end.

His own impressions he writes as follows:-

The Burmese are of the Mongolian type and are Buddhists, and for this reason they have no true idea of God. It is difficult to make them understand, for in their language they seem to have no word that rightly expresses our idea of God. But they are a simple people, and their temples are all open to visitors. They are not bigoted as are, Hindus and Muhammadans. But the Hindus here not only attend meetings themselves but bring their wives with them.

Then he adds:-

I do not see as others seem to see what a great work is going on among the people.

The beginning of 1919 marks a great event in the Sadhu's career, for not only did he make his long journey to China and Japan, but on January 2 he found himself in Singapore amidst a people whose common language was English, and there was no one who could translate from Hindustani for him. Immediately he resolved to use English, and from that day his work was almost entirely done in that language. Only a few months before some important engagements in South India had been dropped for lack of an interpreter, so that it is not surprising that those who were praying that his work in these distant lands might be effective, felt that their prayers were answered when they heard that the Sadhu was fearlessly speaking in English.

From Singapore he went to China, where he stayed a short time. Bishop Maloney gave him a note of introduction to a Japanese Bishop, and after a few meetings he left China, with the promise to spend a little time on his way back, and took ship to Japan. When he reached that country and heard the Japanese speaking in English he felt much encouraged. Thus the great barrier of language which had so often hampered and distressed him is broken down, and he thanks God who has enabled him to witness to the ends of the earth in this wonderful way.

Chapter 29
"Called, Chosen, Faithful"

"They that are with Him are called, chosen, faithful."-
Rev.16:14.

In Japan he was much impressed with the materialism of the people. He felt that there was a deep indifference to religion, and that appeals to the spiritual nature produced little effect, while the greed of money, love of power, and the terrible immorality prevailing, struck a chill of horror through his heart. The national religion appeared to have little hold on the people, and he saw temples fuller of visitors and guides than of worshippers. The rush and hurry of life distressed him. A friend in Yokohama wrote:-

> He spoke once to the foreign community and we were all struck with his apt illustrations, and when he could be persuaded to tell the story of his conversion, it impressed us as a modern version of St. Paul's.

Another writer adds:-

> Few could listen to the story of the Sikh lad who sought so earnestly after truth without their deepest feelings being stirred. St. Paul, after he had seen the heavenly vision, could not but testify to it. "Now I not only know about Christ; I have seen Him," says this Sadhu of the twentieth century; and as he tells the story, you feel with him the surprise he felt when suddenly Christ with wounded hands stood before him.

While from Tokyo came yet another letter from a missionary in which he said:-

His clear putting of spiritual issues was very striking. His word had a spiritual authority behind it. He was our guest here and afterwards joint guest with us in Pekin.

The Rev. Takaharu Takamatsu, Japanese Pastor at Okasaki, wrote:-

He inspired many American missionaries resident in Kyoto, but the native ministers were even more inspired, I think.

A young Japanese who is in the senior class of the Third National College, Kyoto, had been coming to my house before the Sadhu's visit. He is studying natural science and his mind is very rationalistic. He was seeking Light and could only see dimly. He was unable to be present at the Sadhu's meetings, but came to my Bible Class when I spoke about him. He was very quiet and hung his head. A few days after he called at 7.30 a.m. to see me on his way to college. His right hand was bandaged. He told me that the previous night he had experienced the power of God.

He awoke at 3.30 a.m. after a very vivid dream, in which his father had forced him to do something against his will. He arose from his bed, and felt within himself a spiritual force at work that exercised the same control over his mind that his father's had physically. He strove to resist it, but the more he fought against it the more he felt obliged to give way. Unconsciously his hands were clasped, and he began to tremble violently until his whole mind and body were filled with joy unspeakable. He wept aloud so that his friends in a neighboring room woke up and came in to see what was the matter.

The young man preached so earnestly that he constantly struck his right hand on the desk until it was hurt.

When he told me this story I explained to him that Christ was calling him, and he must confess Him and tell others of his experience.

That evening, returning from College with two students, one a medical friend and the other a renegade Christian, he began to speak very earnestly about the Savior, when a crowd gathered round to hear. The renegade Christian listening to his words wept out his repentance, and said that for the first time he had understood Christianity and would follow Christ. Thus is the Sadhu's short visit bearing fruit in the lives of our people.

Japanese Christians have been called to consider earnestly such great matters as single-mindedness and purity of aspiration after union with God; that prayer is not merely asking benefits but entering into communion with God; and that full self-surrender to Christ means a glad willingness to do and suffer His will even if it lead to the sacrifice of life itself. One such says:-

Because he has gone all the way possible in some directions he speaks with authority as a messenger from God.

A Japanese lady, after hearing of how Sundar found Christ, exclaimed:-

A dear friend of mine, deeply dissatisfied with the old teaching (of his own religion), struggled hard to find light, but failing he flung himself into a waterfall when he was but eighteen years of age. Alas! my friend knew nothing of Christ, had no one to go to in his darkness; the ground slipped away from under his feet, and so he ended his life.

For the help of such as these Sundar Singh went to Japan.

In China the Sadhu found the people still with a love and reverence for their ancient faiths, and declares them capable of high spiritual development. In both Japan and China he was amazed to find how by reason of there being no caste distinctions as in India, the acceptance of Christianity was made so much simpler from a social standpoint.

A missionary wrote from Peking:-

In Peking his coming was most timely, and I trust has given the Peking Cathedral congregation a great lift. It was good to see a Methodist translating for the Sadhu in the Cathedral. It was fuller than it ever had been on a Sunday, and at the Monday meeting-a suddenly announced service-the Cathedral was again full. His way of putting things in English is after the model of the Gospels.

On the Sunday evening he preached to Europeans and Americans in the Union Church. From Peking he wrote saying he was in excellent health and enjoying the real cold of the fine climate.

At Hankow influenza was raging, but he was able to do some work. The son of the great missionary, Hudson Taylor, translated for him into Chinese. He then passed further into Shansi Province to the place where in 1900 many missionaries were martyred along with numbers of Chinese. When he heard how bravely they suffered, and how even boys had stood firm as they watched their parents done to death before they were called on to suffer, his soul was stirred to its profoundest depths.

He arrived unexpectedly at Nanking, so that no preparations had been made for him. The Rev. J. G. Magee went to the station to meet a friend, and finding the Sadhu there he took him home. Mr. Magee says :-

He preached at a chapel recently opened, and the people were much impressed by him -personally, and by his striking message with its unique illustrations. They are still talking about him. Just today a young Chinaman said to me, without my raising the subject, that the Church members believed in Sundar Singh. He meant that Sundar Singh was leading the Christian life more fully than he had ever seen.

In the afternoon he spoke to a group of new converts, and at night to a meeting of missionaries on "Witnessbearing." "You would not need to be told of the effect of his words on such a subject to such an audience," the writer adds.

His own witness-bearing in those regions then came to an end, and within a short time he found himself amongst friends in Madras, and with their help speedily reached Simla. From there he went on to Sabathu, when he once more occupied the room where fourteen years before, after much prayer, he had put on the sadhu garb and made his solemn vow to follow Christ wherever He led.

At Kotgarh he was laid up with a wounded foot, and his journey into Tibet, much to his regret, was delayed. But on July 4 he was well, and once more turned his back on civilization and friends, and started on his lonely journey to the frozen highlands of his chosen field of labor, where amongst the great solitudes of the snow-clad Himalayas he again held high converse with God.

Even those windswept plateau of Tibet, whose scanty populations refuse his message and drive him forth hungering into the wilderness, provide for him those great experiences about which he is so reticent, but which prove him to be specially called of God and cared for by Him when human help fails. For months together the Sadhu has wandered alone in regions seldom trodden by the foot of man, and has learnt to love the mountain peaks where he beholds God's mighty works and often hears His "still small voice."

Amidst such scenes Sundar Singh has not only seen visions, but has gathered power for his ministry among the multitudes of the plains. And while his sensitive soul turns with longing to the wider spaces where he can be alone with God, he has walked through countless temptations and still retains through them all the unspoiled sweetness and simplicity his lonely life of hardship for Christ has given him.

Chapter 30
Christ Sent Me To Preach The Gospel

"Christ sent me ... to preach the gospel." -1 Corinthians 1:17.

"I have fully preached the gospel of Christ. Yea, so have I strived to preach the gospel, where Christ was not named . . . as it is written, To whom He was not spoken of, they shall see; and they that have not heard shall understand."-Romans 15:19-21.

It is an acknowledged fact that some sermons are more power-ful in print than when delivered. The reverse, however, is even more true, for many really great sermons with far-reaching results would make but a poor show on paper. The desire has been ex-pressed in several quarters for the sermons of Sadhu Sundar Singh to appear in book form, and a Tamil edition of such a book has been published. But those who know him best, and the true value of his work, feel doubtful as to whether such a book can possibly do him justice.

Sadhu Sundar Singh is a good preacher; he loses no time in figures of speech, wastes no words on fine phrases. He is direct, clear, concise. Needless to say, he is in dead earnest, and leaves no single hearer in doubt as to the object he has in view. No hesitation in delivery or haziness of expression mars the effect of what he has to say. He never appears without a message straight from God, and his clear voice carries that message to the remotest limits of his audience, however large that audience may be. A tense silence and strained attention witness to the power with which he speaks. His calm and yet humble dignity of manner, as he stands with his small Urdu Testament in his clasped hands, is strangely at variance with his impassioned language and vigor of delivery. Not for one moment does any dullness creep in to give opportunity to heedless hearers to stare about.

Sadhu Sundar Singh

Constantly in parable or from actual personal experience, Sadhu Sundar Singh illustrates what he has to say, and always aptly and strikingly. In lecturing to non-Christians he contends that religion is not a matter of argument but of experience, and proves very conclusively before he has done that this is so. However mixed his audience may be, none can go away without the deep impression of having heard the truth. Lovers of Jesus Christ are fortified in their faith, the careless are brought suddenly to a standstill and made to reconsider their position. Thoughtful non-Christians are brought face to face with the question whether Christ has any claim on them, and as a result many have been brought to the feet of the Savior.

The real significance of the preaching of the Sadhu lies in his triumphant reaffirmation of the eternal things of spiritual life. The charm of the message has brought new life to many Christians who before his coming had scarcely felt the vital power of Christ in their own lives, and to whom religion was more or less a lifeless thing. For many of these the first flush of zeal and devotion for Christ had passed away, and the pressure of the world had blurred the heavenly vision.

But Sadhu Sundar Singh, coming fresh from the continual communion he holds with his Lord, stands amongst men in his Sadhu's robes, filled with a message so persuasive, so insistent, so attractive, that once again is felt the power and the sweetness of a Savior well-nigh forgotten. He draws his life from God's unfailing springs of joy, and communicates something of that joy to those who see and hear him, until they too are fired with desire to drink at the same fountain and share the same bliss.

His message to Christians is strong and impressive. It is urgent and compelling, pointing to higher and nobler ideals of living, which his hearers must heed or be left worse off than before he came.

In preaching to non-Christians he never attacks their religion or uses unbrotherly terms of reproach. But he fearlessly testifies to his own failure after long and painful search to find peace, joy, and satisfaction, apart from God's great revelation in Jesus Christ. Neither argument nor philosophy, but the inspiration which comes from the simple yet powerful testimony to the power of God to redeem from sin, is his method of drawing non-Christians to the feet of Christ.

The Sadhu goes back to foundation things: God's love; Christ's witness in life and death to that love; the unfailing power of that love to save all who accept it; and supremely Christ and His cross are his theme. He speaks of One he intimately knows; One whose power he has never ceased to experience from the hour when that One appeared to him as a boy; One who is his companion day and night, and for whom he has given up everything that life can offer. His hearers are conscious that before them stands a man who is Living Christ as well as preaching Him.

Sadhu Sundar Singh's own personality carries weight with his message. At one of his early meetings in the South, when his address was over, he sat down before the translation was completed, and it then became most difficult for the good translator to keep the attention of the audience to the end. At later meetings he remained standing until the translation was finished, when not an eye was turned away for a moment. It is himself and his message combined that is powerful to influence those who receive that message from his lips.

The writer of Ecce Homo says:-

The first step towards a good disposition is for a man to form a strong personal attachment. Let the object of that attachment be a person of striking and conspicuous goodness. He will ever have before his eyes an ideal of what he himself may become. Example is a personal influence.

The Sadhu wherever he goes is able to awaken this feeling of strong personal attachment, and this power he uses entirely to draw men to Christ. The crowds that constantly linger round that they may catch sight of him, and the honorable titles often accorded him voluntarily in places where he goes (such as Mahatma and Swami, indicating a partaker of the Divine nature), witness to this spirit of personal devotion. Devout Christians realize that if the Sadhu can awaken such feelings, how much greater loyalty and devotion may spring from the appeal of Jesus Christ Himself. And thus by his personality he leads men upwards to the one source of spiritual life.

Many young men in the South have desired to become his disciples; but the advice of the Sadhu to all such is that they should serve God where they are and amongst those around them.

His chief work, the work he recognizes as that specially given him by God, lies beyond the limit of ordinary churches, amongst those inaccessible to their influence and suasion. "To the churches he comes to impart a deeper glow and sterner purpose, but he passes on his way without tabulating results, only leaving behind a burning message and an inspiring memory. His simplicity is a rebuke to all selfish love of the world, and his presentation of Christianity is calculated to correct the erroneous idea that it is only a religion suited to westerners in which India can have no share."

In Tibet, amidst a hostile people and in constant danger, this humble servant of Christ is carrying "the message which is the heart of his own life." Alone, in cold and hunger, without a place to lay his head, but filled with an absorbing passion for his Master and for the souls "sitting in darkness and in the shadow of death," Sundar Singh toils over the snow-strewn wastes. That, solitary figure does not pass from His sight as it does from ours, for assuredly Christ walks beside him, works and suffers with him.

From those lonely heights comes back the echo of his own words, "How ashamed we shall be when we meet in the presence of God and before saints and martyrs, if we do not live real Christian lives here!" These are not new words, but as Mr. Stokes once said, "When they come from the lips of one who has long suffered hunger, cold, imprisonment, and persecution for his Master, they fall upon our ears with an awful authority and power."

O God, O kinsman loved, but not enough!
O Man, with eyes majestic after death,
Whose feet have toiled along our pathways rough,

Whose lips drawn human breath!
Come, lest this heart should, cold and cast away,
Die, ere the guest adored she entertain-

Lest eyes which never saw Thine earthly day
Should miss Thy heavenly reign.

THE MESSAGE OF THIS BOOK

This little book lays no claim to being a life of Sadhu Sundar Singh, or even a record of his labors. It attempts to lay bare the secret of the singularly beautiful character of a deeply religious soul, and seeks to extend as well as to keep in mind the magnetic influence of a wholly consecrated life.

If in any measure it shows how one good man in preaching and living Christ so presents Him to the world as to "draw all men unto Him," and if other hearts are stirred to a deeper devotion to Christ and so catch something of the Sadhu's spirit, its purpose will be served.

It is a great joy to render this small tribute to the amazing power of Sadhu Sundar Singh to turn men to Christ, and it is offered to the reader by one who has experienced that power, in the hope and with the prayer that its message may be blessed of God to all who will receive it. — R. J. P.

JESUS SAID -"I, if I be lifted up . . . will draw all men unto Myself."

Sirdar Sher Singh made various attempts from time to time to win back his son, and the Urdu letter on the next page is one of them. In it he urged that Sundar should marry. "I do not want to ask you what you think, but I order you to get married immediately. Can you not serve your guru, Christ, in a married state? . . . Does the Christian religion teach disobedience to parents?" He then goes on to say he will leave large sums of money to Sundar if only he will carry on the family name, and also chides him for living in poverty and dressing so poorly.

Appendix

1. The Sadhu and His Father

In his reply Sundar respectfully reminds his father of the definite call he has had to live the true sadhu life in which marriage is impossible, and that when he became a Christian he gave up all thought of earthly wealth, adding, "You are wise and experienced and can do as seems best; as for me, having once put my hand to the plough I will not look back."

After fourteen years of unswerving, loyalty to Christ Sadhu's many prayers were gloriously answered when he visited his old home in October, 1919. His aged father welcomed him with joy, and during the few days they were together Sundar had the great happiness of hearing that his father had at last given his heart to the Savior who had so transformed his son. Sirdar Sher Singh earnestly desired baptism at his son's hands, but, believing that Christ had sent him not to baptize, and in view of the fact that thousands throughout India have been refused the same favor, Sadhu felt that he could not accede to this most natural request.

It is a touching testimony to this happy reunion that Sirdar Sher Singh has made provision for his son to go on a great preaching tour to the West, and by the time this book is in the hands of English readers, Sadhu Sundar Singh will be laboring in their midst.

2. Travelling In Tibet

Upon his return from Tibet last autumn the Sadhu wrote the following account of his journey:-

In the beginning of July, 1919, I left Kotgarh for Tibet in company with a Christian whose Tibetan name is Thaniyat. The Tibetan frontier is nearly 180 miles beyond Kotgarh, and preaching in Hirath, Rcmpur, Bushaher, Goura, Sachan, Chaura, Tranda, Pounta, Hachar, Kodgaon, Karcha, and Kcmphcran, we arrived at Yangpa, which is the first town of Tibet. From here for forty miles the country is entirely jungle anJ there is not a single village or dwelling-place, only here and there a flock of sheep and shepherd come into view. We remained in this wilderness five nights; one night we spent under a tree and another night in a cave; for from now onwards for a long distance there arc no trees because of the extreme cold and great height, so that scarcely a blade of grass springs up anywhere. As far as the eye can reach there is nothing but bare mountains and plateaux.

The Cold Of The Mountains

At a height of 16,000 feet we slept out on the open plain when the cold was so intense that all feeling went out of the body and we became numb all over. The whole of one night the rain fell in torrents, and in the bitter cold we had to sit all night under an umbrella. This place is a very dangerous one, for many people have died there in the snow.

On July 15 we came to Hangpu La Pass which is nearly 19,000 feet high, where we saw the corpses of three men who had died from the terrific cold. At this great height we could scarcely draw our breath, our heads and lungs were filled with pain, and the beating of our hearts sounded in our ears. Here is a great glacier on which many people have lost their lives, and their bodies have never been recovered to this day. Thanks be to God we passed through this awful place in safety.

On July 16 we arrived at a Tibetan village called Mudh, where the headman received us into his house kindly, and that night he invited an important Lama to dine with us, who understood Hindustani, and we preached the Word. He listened with great attention and pleasure and did not prevent others from hearing also. The next day we went on to Taling and Sangnam and again from there to Inamb, Kveling, Kuring, and Saling, and still further on to Sideng, Sara, Koze, and Rangrig, and preached in every place we passed through.

We then came to Koo Gunra, where there is a large temple. In the building connected with it some 400 Lamas reside, the Head Lama having been sent direct from Lhasa. This Head Lama is connected with Lhasa and was appointed through the Lama Tashi. With him we remained two days and he gave us little trouble, although he was very keen on discussing religion with us.

In Perils Of Rivers

In Tibet there are not only one but many kinds of hardships and difficulties. There are no roads, and although there are many streams and rivers there are no bridges to cross them, and the water is always as cold as ice. Wherever the water was shallow enough we were able to swim across, but sometimes the current was so strong and the river bed so full of rocks that swimming became impossible. One day in swimming across the river Morang I reached the other bank with great difficulty, for the water was so intensely cold that my whole body became stiff and numb. At Thaniyat I fell and went under the water three times and with great straining and difficulty I got out of that river, a river in which many men have sunk never to rise again.

Food is another difficult problem in Tibet. There is nothing to eat and drink in most places except campa or sattu (fried barley flour) and a kind of tea which is mixed with salt and butter. Again and again the fried barley was so bad that even horses and asses would not eat it. In all these difficulties there was this great comfort, that this was the cross of Christ, and was necessary for the salvation of souls. For me Christ forsook heaven and took upon

Himself the burden of the Cross, so that if I have left India to come into Tibet on His behalf to claim souls for Him, it is not a great thing to do; but if I had not come it would have been a dreadful thing, for this is a divine command.

The Sin Of Washing Clothes

Tibetan houses are very small and exceedingly dirty. They are built of stones and mud, and the smell of the people is unbearable. In the village of Lara I saw a man who was quite black with dirt, and I think he could not have had a bath for fifteen years at least. The people's clothes, although made of white wool, from filth look as if they were made of black leather, because they never wash' their clothes. In the village of Kiwar we washed our clothes in a stream and everybody came to see.

They were struck with amazement that we should be doing such a thing. An important Lama said, "It is all right for sinful men to wash their clothes, but for good people to do so is very bad."

Although there has been much difficulty in this journey, yet it has been less than at other times. The Lamas in some places received us well and gave us salted tea and fried barley flour to eat. One day they saw that I was uncomfortable because my hair had grown very long. Having no scissors to cut it, four Lamas came along bringing with them an instrument with which they are accustomed to shear the sheep, and with this they cut my hair.

In Perils Of Robbers

From Kiwar we went to Chikan and then on to Skite, Hause, Sasar, and Pangre, and had fine opportunities for preaching, but there were very few dwelling-places, and great fear of many thieves and robbers. One good man said, "You cannot go without a gun or sword through this place, because many men have been killed here." I replied, "I have only a blanket and this Bible-the sword of God-and the Lord of Life is with me; He will save me."

Therefore, thanks be to Him we went through that dreadful place preaching amongst murderers and doing His work, yet not a single thing happened to give us trouble of any kind. In this place were men whose legs or arms had been cut off by murderers and thieves, but God with great might brought us safely through.

Tibetan Religious Practices

Although Tibetans are horribly dirty and often stupidly ignorant they are also very religious. In some districts the custom is for the eldest son to remain at home to look after the property, and all the remaining sons become Lamas or priests. Many people write upon paper or cloth, texts from their sacred books (of which there are 108 volumes called Khangiryur tangiryur) and hang them as flags above the roofs of their houses. Also they write the sacred words OM MANE PADME HUM many times on paper, and place the roll inside a brass wheel which they continually turn round and round. Some fasten them on watermills, sometimes writing them on stones which they place in a heap and go round them. These, as it were, are their prayers, by which they believe they will gain forgiveness of sins and obtain blessing.

Concerning the true God these people know nothing, but in their religion they have a kind of Trinity which is called Sangi Kunchek, or Buddha God; Lama Kunchek, or Priest God; and Ghho Kunchek, or Scripture God. Buddhism entered Tibet about A.D. 629 in the time of King Shang Taing Suganpo, and Lamaism was founded in A.D. 749 by Padmasambhave, who started the first monastery near Lhasa.

In the year A.D. 1640 a Mongolian prince, Gusari Khan, conquered Tibet and made a present to the Grand Lama of Drepung Monastery with the title of Dalai or Ocean who thus became the first King-Priest and is known as the Dalai Lama. His name was Magwan Lobang. Being very ambitious and wanting to combine the rule of the State with the Church, he declared himself an incarnation of the famous Chcnrezing Avalokitesvara, the tutelary deity of Tibet. The Tibetans were no doubt delighted to have as ruler an incarnation of such a divinity, and the scheme worked well, but in order not to offend the older, and in one sense superior, Lama of Troshi Shumpo, he declared this Lama an incarnation of Amitabha. Thus Dalai Lama declared himself an incarnation of Avalokitesvara, while the Tashi Lama is an incarnation, of a higher deity, yet it is an impassive deity who cannot meddle with worldly affairs which are left to his spiritual son Avalokitesvara, represented by the Dalai Lama of Tibet.

The Hermits Of Tibet

The lives of many Tibetan hermits are very wonderful. They shut themselves in a dark room. Some do this for months, and some for years, and some for the whole of life. They are so shut away that they never see the sun and never come out of doors, but always sitting in the dark they continue turning a prayer-wheel in their hand just as if they were living in a grave. In these small rooms is a tiny window or hole through which the people pass food to these hermits. *I tried to get into conversation with them, but never had a proper opportunity, and all I could do was to throw some Scripture portion through the hole in the hope they might read it if ever they came out.

This lesson I learnt from them: that if these people will end lire such suffering in order to attain Nirvana, in which there is no future life or heavenly happiness nor any hope, believing that salvation lies in exterminating desire and spirit and life, how much more shall we not take up the cross with joy for Christ-the joy of our entrance into eternal life and of His great service who has given and will give us all things?

In this country, because of the snow and intense cold, there is only one harvest in the year, which is sown in May and reaped in September. In some places wheat, and in others mustard, are sown. Some of the jungly country is beautiful with flowers; wild onions and even gram are sometimes seen. But alas! all sorts of evil customs and horrible wickedness prevail, the very mention of which is impossible here.

In Journeys Often

We went to a number of other places and worked amongst the people, returning by another way through Kyamo, Hal, Maling, Khurik, Sumling, Phiti, and Boldar. My desire was to go alone to Kailash and Rasar, but this year my journey to Tibet was greatly delayed. Between July 30 and August 9 on that side the mountains become thickly covered with snow, and there are many rivers and streams, although some rivers have bridges of ice stretching across them. But there are many rivers which have no bridges at all and they are too dangerous for swimming, so that it seemed as if every way was closed, and there was no choice but to return. May God grant that in the coming April I may journey to every place. If I had remained until September the heavy snows would have effectually barred my return, and by October it would have been impossible to reach India.

The Firstfruit Of Coming Harvest

This time I went forty-eight stages into Tibet, each day being about ten miles. I should like to tell of every place I visited, but there is no time for more than this brief account. Those Christians who live in Tibet itself and on the borders, are by God's grace well as far as I am able to find out. There is a boy in Tsering who knows Hindustani well and was very desirous of returning to India, with me but his mother prevented him. I trust another year he will come with me, and having received further training may become a good preacher amongst his own people in Tibet, so that the seed of God's Word which has been sown on this journey by His grace may spring up and in His own time bear much fruit. Amen.
Sundar Singh.

3. Tibet And The Great War

While the first edition of this book was going through the press English papers published the following:-

> "Tibet, the most solitary of the hermit nations, has come forward with an offer of a hundred thousand men to help fight the battles of democracy on the European front. Our awed imaginations have lingered over the impossible terrors of the road to Lhasa, forbidden on pain of death to outsiders. The barred doors swing wide on rusty hinges, and the Grand Lama, most secluded of the world's monarchs, steps into the fast-running currents of twentieth century history as the friend and defender of democracy."

The natural prayer of the Christian is that this closed land may now open its doors to the Gospel, and that Sadhu Sundar Singh may "see of the travail of his soul" in bringing Tibet to the feet of Christ.

4. The Sikhs

The Sikh States lie in the Punjab, roughly speaking between the rivers Ganges and Indus, and are bounded on the north by the mountainous region that separates them from Tibet and the Chinese Empire. The two capitals are Amritsar and Lahore.

Nanak was the first of the Gurus or Teachers of the Sikhs. He was born at Rayapur in 1469. From childhood he was inclined to devotion and indifferent to worldly concerns. His father sought to divert his mind from religious things, and on one occasion sent him to transact some business for him, which was to result in financial profit. On the way Nanak met some hungry fakirs, and divided his father's money between them, observing, "The gain of this world is transient. I wish to relieve these poor men and thus obtain that gain which is eternal." After partaking of food the fakirs entered into a long discourse upon the unity of God, with which Nanak was greatly delighted. Returning to his home, his father asked what profit he had brought, and receiving the reply that he had fed the poor, his father abused and even struck him. Rai Bolar, the ruler of the district, hearing of this, interdicted Nanak's father from ever again treating him in this way, and he himself humbly bowed in veneration before Nanak.

Nanak then, adopting the saffron robe, began to practice the austerities of a holy man, and soon became celebrated for the goodness of his life and character. He travelled to many Hindu holy places, and even to Mecca itself, in order to purify the worship of both Hindus and Muhammadans. Wherever he journeyed, he preached the doctrine of the unity and omnipresence of God. Born in a province where these two races were utterly opposed to each other, he yet strove to blend them in one harmonious peace, and to bring them back to a simple and pure religion.

Nanak taught that devotion was due to one God, and idol worship must be banished, his object being to reform, not to destroy, existing religions. Before his death his followers had become a distinct sect, and were known as "Sikhs," which means Disciples. In all his writing Nanak borrowed indiscriminately from the Shastras and Qur'an. Many of the chapters of the Adi Granth were written by Nanak and were in verse. Nanak desired to abolish all caste distinctions, and place all men on an equality. He also declared that the most acceptable offerings to God are morning praise and the presentation of the body to him.

After the death of Nanak other leaders followed to the number of ten, the two most famous of these being Arjun and Govind Singh. A bitter persecution of the new sect by Muhammadans converted a harmless religious people into a great military commonwealth, determined to avenge the sufferings they had endured. The martyrdom of their pontiff Arjun turned a hitherto inoffensive sect into a band of fanatical warriors. Har Govind, one of their leaders at the time, gave to all his followers the honorable name of "Singh" (Lion), and the order that no Singh should allow his hair to be cut was issued at the same time.

Govind Singh, the tenth and last of the great Sikh leaders or pontiffs, wrote a large part of the tenth book of the Granth, and held a place in the esteem of his followers at least equal to Nanak himself. Under Govind Singh the Sikhs assumed the character and rank of a military nation. Before his death he made the promise that whenever five Sikhs should meet together he would be present amongst them.

The temples of the Sikhs are generally plain buildings with a flat roof and sufficiently large to hold a number of worshippers, who stand during service. The forms of prayer and praise are simple. Portions of the Granth are read or sung, and the priest exhorts the people to "meditate on the Book." Daily worship is performed by pious Sikhs and portions of their scriptures are read. Sikhs believe that they were placed by their last and most revered pontiff Govind under the peculiar care of God.

5. Some of the Sadhu's Illustrations

The Sadhu's addresses go to the root of fundamental things such as repentance, faith, sacrifice. Almost every point is illustrated by some parable from nature or some actual experience. The following are examples:

Humility.-A poor Indian of the sweeper caste became a Christian, and a high caste man who knew him was much struck by the great change in him. "You used to come and sweep my house; you had no education, and yet I cannot help honoring you. What has changed you?"

The sweeper tried to explain the new life that had come to him, but still the high caste man did not understand. Especially he wondered at one thing: "You are so good, and yet you are not proud!"

"Why should I be proud?" asked the sweeper. "When Christ rode an ass into Jerusalem, people brought clothes and laid them upon the road. Yet the feet of our Lord did not tread on them, only the ass walked over them. Who ever heard of such honor being done to the feet of an ass? It was only because the ass carried Christ. When He had done riding the ass, the beast was of no account. So I am of no account, only I am as it were bearing Christ, and it is Him you honor. If He left me I should be nothing at all."

Union with and Life in God.- From our own experience we do become united with God, yet we do not become God. If a piece of cold iron is placed in a hot fire it will glow because the fire is in it. Yet we cannot say that the iron is fire or the fire is iron. So in Jesus Christ we retain our identity; He in us and we in Him, but with our own individuality.

Again we breathe air, yet man is not air nor is the air man. So we breathe by prayer the Holy Spirit of God, but we are not God. Some time ago I saw two villages in the Himalayas that were separated by an impassable mountain. The direct distance between the two was not great, but the journey round took travellers a week to accomplish. A man in one of the villages determined to make a tunnel through this mountain, declaring he would give his life to do it if necessary. He started on the work, and in the attempt he did actually lose his life. When I heard of it I thought this mountain was like the wall of our sin keeping us away from God. Jesus Christ came and made a Living Way by giving His life. He gave His life of His own will, and the way is open to all who unreservedly accept Him as their Savior.

The Better Part.-Once, when I was crossing the mountains I met a girl. She was of good family and was on pilgrimage, and her bare feet were bleeding. In answer to my question she said, "I am looking for rest and peace, and I hope to get them before I get to the end of this pilgrimage. If I do not I shall drown myself." I saw she was in earnest. I thought how strange it is that people who are born Christians and have these great gifts without taking all this trouble should care so little for them, while this wealthy girl had given up her home and all she cared most for to seek salvation. She did not find peace on that pilgrimage, but she met a missionary who told her about Christ. I saw her afterwards and she told me that she had found all and more than she had sought, adding, "Men may kill me if they like. I have found that better part that shall never be taken away from me."

Ye are the Light of the World.-The wick of a lamp must burn and lose itself in order that the light may shine. The wick is between the oil and the flame. There may be plenty of oil, but if there be no wick there can be no light. So to give light to others we must be ready to sacrifice ourselves.

Ye are the Salt of the Earth.-If salt is to be of use it must be dissolved. So long as it remains in a dry lump it cannot give flavor to our food, but when it is dissolved every grain of rice has its proper taste and the food is good. So with individual Christians; they must always be giving of themselves. They may seem to disappear and be lost, but that is not actually the case. They live in the lives of those for whom they have given themselves, and their influence remains.

Safe in Christ.-We are small, the attraction of the earth is great. But powerful as is the force of the earth, when we grasp anything in our hand the attraction of the earth cannot draw it away. So when we are in the hand of Christ earthly things can have no power over us, for in His keeping we are safe.

God in Christ.-Hindus are very fond of saying that God is in everything. I once came to a river which I had to cross. There was no boat to carry me over, and I stood wondering how it could be managed. Then a man called my attention to a deflated water-skin, and said that was the only way to get across. So we inflated it with air and I crossed over in safety. Then the thought came to me that there was plenty of air all round me, but it was incapable of helping me in my difficulty until it was confined in the narrow space of the water-skin. So it is as unreasonable to deny the necessity of the Incarnation of Christ as to declare that the air-filled leather boat was of no use to help in crossing that river.

Our Helplessness.-The little chicken in its shell lives in a very circumscribed and narrow world of its own. It is receiving its mother's warmth and care all the time, but it is unconscious of them because it cannot see or know her. It has wings, but they are closely folded and it cannot use them. So it is with us until God calls us out into His abundant life.

Abundant Life.-I once knew a man who was very sick and could not rise from his bed. His house caught fire, and he strove to get out, but he had no strength. He cried aloud, and with all his small stock of strength he struggled to get out of the burning room. He had life, but it was not enough to save him, and so he was burnt to death. Another man came by before the fire was over, and he was able to put it out, because he had abounding strength, but he was too late to save the sick man. Another man I knew was very ill, and he had lost all sense of taste. Pleasant dishes of food were prepared for him, but he disliked them and would not eat them, and so he got weaker and weaker. Many Christians have lost their taste for spiritual things. They have life, but there is not abundant life. Buddhism and Hinduism teach many good things, but only Christ offers this abundant life, and it is only by experience that anyone can really understand the difference between life and this abundant life which is the gift of Christ.

The Necessity of Suffering.-A silkworm was struggling out of the cocoon, and an ignorant man saw it battling as if in pain, so he went and helped it to get free, but very soon after it fluttered and died. The other silkworms that struggled out without help suffered, but they came out into full life and beauty with wings made strong for flight by their battle for fresh existence.

The Water of Life.-Some time ago a party of men were travelling in Tibet. One of them became very thirsty, but there was no water. As they went on they saw some pools surrounded by marshy ground, where the thirsty man determined to quench his thirst. Those who knew the nature of the country begged him to wait until they should reach a safe place, but he would not listen, and said he would take owe. He plunged ahead towards a pool, and filling his hands began to drink. He called to his friends to tell them he had got his heart's desire, and even as he spoke he began to sink in the morass. Soon he was half buried, and no one could venture near to draw him out, and his companions looked helplessly on as he sank and at length he disappeared, miserably perishing as so many do who drink the water of a sinful life.

Appendix to the Fourth American Edition

A WORLD EVANGELIST

"The glorious gospel of the blessed God was committed (to my trust. And I thank Jesus Christ who hath enabled me, for that he counted m faithful, putting me into the ministry, . . . that in me first Jesus Christ might show forth all long suffering, for a pattern to them who should hereafter believe on Him to everlasting life." 1 Timothy 1:11-17.

Going West.-- Towards the end of 1919 a few of the Sadhu's friends heard that he was contemplating a journey to England, but when early in 1920 he sent them word that it was imminent, the news came almost as a bolt from the blue. Arrangements were so hurried that little could be done in preparation, and many of his friends were in ignorance of his plans right up to the time of his departure. One reason for this was that the Sadhu desired to go West unheralded in order that God who had called him to go, should be free to open doors of service which elaborate arrangements might have rendered impossible. He had his desire, for by the time his friends were able to write to England he was on his way thither.

While numbers of people were anxiously awaiting passages the Sadhu obtained one immediately, getting an entire cabin to himself, thus allowing privacy for devotion and rest. The night previous to his departure a farewell meeting was held in Bombay. One present said,

"To many matter-of-fact natures the thoughts of a mystic are unfathomable . . . but to those who heard him speak . . . one lasting impression remains, that of a soul that has seen Christ face to face, and to whom there can be but one object in life Christ Himself. Few could listen to the story of the Sikh lad who sought so earnestly after truth, without their deepest feelings being stirred. St. Paul after he had seen the heavenly vision, could but testify to it.

"Now I not only know about Christ; I have seen Him," says Sadhu of the twentieth century; and as he tells the story, you feel with him the surprise he felt when after his earnest prayer . . . suddenly Christ stood before him."

The Sadhu left Bombay by the "City of Cairo" on January 16th and after an uneventful voyage landed at Liverpool on February 10th.

Amongst Quakers. The Sadhu began his work in England first at the request of the Society of Friends; he went from the north to Birmingham to be the guest of Principal Hoyland. In speaking to the students of the Friends' Missionary Training College his somewhat limited vocabulary in English embarrassed him. One student said that the Sadhu had cleared his doubts with regard to the Atonement. Like his Master he lives above all wrangling sects and creeds, and the Sadhu's appeal should reach the West through this very channel, since regardless of dividing opinions and doctrines he serves all, ceaselessly calling men back to visions of Christ so transcending all man-made divisions that have for so long held back the visible church from claiming a sin-wracked world for her Lord.

Amongst the Cowley Fathers.-- In India the Sadhu had experienced much sympathetic kindness from the Cowley Fathers in Poona, and they gave him an introduction to their Father Superior at Oxford. So from Birmingham he went down to Oxford, and both there and in London he was their guest. In Oxford he preached in the Church of St. John the Evangelist, spoke at Mansfield College, Somerville College for Women, and in the far-famed Hall of Balliol College to a packed audience of undergraduates. Passing on to London he was for a few days the guest of Mr. Barber, and his first sermon in the metropolis was preached at the

Blackheath Congregational Church, which for so long has been associated with the School for the Sons of Nonconformist Missionaries.

By that time the Cowley Fathers had completed their arrangements, and a small handbill was circulated inviting attendance at his meetings in which it was said,

"In meetings which he has recently addressed in Oxford he made a deep impression by his transparent devotion to Christ, and the freshness and simplicity of his message."

So hurried, however, were the arrangements that over large areas of London it was difficult to get news of his program. The next few days large numbers crowded to St. Matthew's Church, Westminster, and St. Bride's Church, Fleet Street. London papers gave accounts of his work, and his picture appeared in many of them. One who was present at St. Bride's spoke of the Sadhu as "an instrument perfected for a purpose" and continued: "Possibly for the first time in City records a preacher from the Far East has come to refresh the religion of the West. There was no scene during the sermon, no sign of emotional stress, but nearly everyone knelt in prayer at the end, an unusual thing in these general congregations and went out very gravely into the rush of Fleet Street."

The Westminster Gazette said of him:

"His smile irradiates a strong Eastern face and when he unbends as with little children, he becomes a winsome personality and immediately wins their confidence. This morning as he entered the little room of the Cowley Fathers I thought I had never seen such a remarkable Eastern figure. His hair and beard are black, and the skin is a wonderfully clear olive. His garb is that of the Indian ascetic, and his tall manly figure adds dignity to the flowing robe. On his feet were sandals, which, however, he discards in his own country.

"'We have our castes in India,' he explained to me, 'our high castes and our low castes, and people do not understand you if you say that having embraced Christianity you belong to this sect or that. They think it is another caste. I am free to go anywhere and there is no barrier of sect.' He is carrying out his principles in England in a notable manner. High Churchmen like Father Bull and Evangelical Church men like the Rev. Cyril Bardesley are associated with his visit. The Bishop of London is to preside over a meeting of London clergy, when Sadhu Sundar Singh will speak. At the same time he is speaking in West minster Chapel for Dr. Jowett, and in the Metropolitan Tabernacle for the Baptists. He is just teaching Western people the true Catholic spirit from Eastern lips."

Amongst the Bishops.-- On March 9 the Sadhu met and talked for an hour with the Archbishop of Canter bury, and the following day he spoke at the Church House, Westminster, to some 700 clergy of the Church of England, including the Archbishop of Canterbury and six Bishops; probably the first occasion when Churchmen of all shades of opinion met together to welcome one to whom sect is nothing, but Christ is all.

Varied Engagements.-- The Sadhu then went to Cambridge, and as at Oxford besides other meetings, he took one for undergraduates at Trinity College. Returning to London he fulfilled some engagements for the Y. M C. A., spoke at the annual meeting of the London City Mission, the Central Missionary Conference for Great Britain, went down to Brighton and thence on to Paris to address the meeting of the Paris Evangelical Missionary Society.

On April 1 he occupied the pulpit of Dr. Jowett at Westminster, who introduced him with the words, "I feel it an exceptional honor to have beside me in my pulpit a native Christian from India who has been so manifestly blessed in Christian work."

The following day, Good Friday, the Sadhu spoke to a packed audience of Christian Endeavourers in the Metropolitan Tabernacle, forever associated with the name of Charles Spurgeon. The London Daily Chronicle in reporting this meeting asks: "How is it that the Sadhu has so manifestly captured the religious world within the short space of six weeks? . . . The secret of this man's power lies in his utter self-abandonment to a high ideal. ... It is surely a token of good that we of the West, who are so obsessed with the materialistic spirit of the age have come in close contact with one who stands for the supremacy of the spiritual."

The Sadhu did some work in Scotland and Ireland, returning to London for the large gatherings usually held there in May. In Albert Hall ten thousand listened to him at the Church Missionary Society's meeting and many could not gain admission. The London Missionary Society's meeting was no less successful, when Dr. Garvie characterized his speaking with the words, 'Without a parable spake he not unto them.' 'His Eastern illustrations and parables have a peculiar charm for Western audiences.' One little child who heard him said, "He talks in parables like Jesus."

To the Sadhu the most interesting of all these meetings was the British and Foreign Bible Society's Annual Meeting. All his Christian life he has felt a deep debt to this noble Society, and when asked to speak he most gladly bore his witness to the power of the Bible in bringing men to Christ. He much appreciated being made an honorary life member of the Bible Society.

In reflecting on the Sadhu's presence in Scotland Dr. Maclean says,

"It is amazing how history repeats itself. Christianity goes through an endless cycle of death and resurrection. Long ago Christianity became a barren field for intellectual feats and it perished. The churches of Cyprian, Tertullian, Augustine were swept out of existence; cathedrals were converted into bar racks. But Christianity is imperishable, and out of the East it will come again. The Sadhu is perhaps the first of the new apostles to rekindle the fire on dying altars.

"To conquer the world one must count the world as nought. Here is a man who asks nothing of the world, and the multitudes throng at his feet. We have for gotten. . . . The church has again to learn the lesson that only they who renounce the world can hope to conquer it. It may be that Sadhu Sundar Singh was sent by God to impress this vital truth upon our hearts and consciences."

In America.-- Dr. Jowett and others introduced the Sadhu to the American people. Curiously enough, when it was known that he was going to America there were good people who feared the result. Sincerely believing that his mission to the States would be more likely to arouse curiosity than accomplish any great spiritual purpose, a number of devout persons met together for prayer in New York to ask for God's overruling providence in the matter.

There was no time for suitable arrangements to be made before the Sadhu's arrival. The Pond Lyceum Bureau offered to arrange a full program covering the States, and venturing the opinion that as a business proposition it would be an even greater success than the one they had carried through for Rabindranath Tagore. They published preliminary announcements, but when the Sadhu realised what it meant he declined to have anything to do with it. The National Bible Institute then made necessary arrangements covering a couple of months, when the Sadhu was due to leave for Australia. For half of that time he was happy in having the companionship of Mr. Frank Buchman of Hartford Theological Seminary, who wrote afterwards, saying,

"I agree with the newspaper reporters of America who interviewed him 'Nearer the Christ than any living man we have seen.' The leading papers gave him ample space. His pictures appeared in the movies, and he was able to reach influential and lay circles in the various cities. He is Spirit taught, and has almost a medium-like gift of sensing people and situations.

"He brings the message of the Supernatural which this age needs. Men simply flocked to hear him that he had scarcely time for his meals. I have just received a letter from the head mistress of a preparatory school. She said there was a veil of light on every boy's face as he left the Sadhu' s meeting. He said a true word when he predicted that America would have no spiritual leaders fifty years hence if she kept up her present pace. He has a practical message for America."

In writing to the pastors of Hartford Bishop Brewster gave one of the chief reasons the Sadhu had in visiting America:

"The Sadhu is a remarkable and significant person in the Christian world today," he writes. "He is specially anxious to counteract the influence of the many Swamis and other people who have been over in Europe and America trying to capture certain types of mind for Theosophy, Hindu Mysticism, etc."

On May 29 the Sadhu was at Union Theological Seminary in New York. Then followed engagements in Hartford, Baltimore, Pittston, Princeton University, Brick Presbyterian Church, and the Marble Collegiate Church (New York), Brooklyn, Philadelphia, Boston and other cities. On June 25 he went to Silver Bay Students' Conference, and spent four days addressing eight hundred students and their leaders. Early in July he was in Chicago, and passed on to Iowa, Kansas and other places, finally arriving at San Francisco, where his journey and work in America ended.

A marconigram [radio telegram] was sent to Honolulu to tell the people that the Sadhu would be passing through en route for Australia, and during the few hours his steamer remained in that port he went ashore to preach. Whilst in America the Sadhu met with several of the chief religious leaders, amongst whom were Dr. Fosdick and Dr. Robert Speer. He was entertained in one place by Mrs. Stokes, the mother of his friend and fellow-sadhu of former days.

On July 20 the Sadhu left America for Australia.

In Australia.-- The steamer spent one day at Honolulu, when Hawaiian, Chinese, Filipinos, Japanese, English and Americans gathered to the number of four hundred to hear the Sadhu. On August 10 he landed in Sydney, and for a week he held meetings in churches, chapels and the University buildings. A Sydney paper, commenting on one meeting, said,

"One could never forget Tuesday morning, August 17th, when the Sadhu walked into the grounds of St. Andrew's Cathedral to address a meeting of 700 clergy and others in the Chapter House. It was the nearest conception one could form of what our Lord must have been like when He walked the streets of the Holy City of old, for the very presence of the Sadhu brought with it an atmosphere of things Christ-like and during the twenty minutes he was speaking there was not a sound. And now he has gone back to his own land, but ere he went he left us a new vision of the Christian Savior."

He spent his thirty-first birthday in Adelaide. In Melbourne

Bishop Langley took the chair at his meeting in a Congregational Chapel, and the Sadhu was told that this was the first occasion that an Anglican Bishop had presided or taken part in a service in a nonconformist place of worship in that city. People of varying creeds in all the towns of Australia where he called seemed to forget their differences, and united to give him a hearty welcome.

At Perth the Sadhu was forcibly taken from the ship and had to arrange to leave by a later steamer. The meetings in the Cathedral and Victoria Hall when the Archbishop of Perth presided, were very large. There was no building large enough to hold the crowds, and overflow meetings had to follow, necessitating his speaking twice following.

On September 25 the Sadhu landed in Bombay. His ship had called at Colombo and he had spoken at a meeting there, but had declined an urgent invitation to remain for further work.

India and Rest.-- In spite of being obliged to speak much at large gatherings the Sadhu is no lover of great crowds, so that his popularity of later years has been a trial to him. Partly because of this and partly because of the need of rest he felt obliged to disappoint his friends in Ceylon, for to stay there would inevitably have meant touring through South India as well, and repeating the experiences of 1918. He therefore continued his journey to Bombay, and proceeded immediately to Sabathu for a period of prayerful quiet and meditation.

Before starting out on his winter campaign he wrote more than two hundred letters during the time he was resting. The remainder of the year was spent in evangelistic work in towns and villages and conferences and conventions in the United Provinces, Chota Nagpur, Bengal and the Panjab.

The early months of 1921 were spent in writing a book entitled "Maktab i Masih" or "The School of Christ." Each chapter dealt with such all-important matters as "The Manifestation of the Presence of God," "Sin and Salvation," "Prayer," "Service," "The Cross and the Mystery of Suffering," "Heaven and Hell": and like his preaching was, as he expressed it, "written in the language of illustration."

Owing to his departure to Tibet the proofs could not be corrected, and the book did not appear until towards the end of 1921, when three separate editions in Urdu, Roman-Urdu and Hindi were published. An English translation in India and also in England gives this book to English-speaking people everywhere.

After the completion of the book Sadhu Sundar Singh made an evangelistic tour in North India, going in May to Khandesh to preach at a large Christian mela [festival], and this was practically his last piece of work before starting for Tibet.

Tibet, 1921.-- The following part-account of his work in Tibet was written by the Sadhu himself in English immediately upon his return, and now appears for the first time: "We started for Tibet in the begin ning of May from Kotgarh by way of Simla and Sabathu. Tibet is about 150 miles from Kotgarh.

At Kulu we had good opportunities to preach the gospel and distribute gospel portions among travellers and the people of villages on the way.

"There are some hot springs in Kulu district; some are good for bathing, and some of them are too hot, so that the water is always boiling. Travellers often put their rice tied up in cloths to boil and the rice is cooked in fifteen minutes. Once a boy fell into these boiling springs, and in a few minutes he was taken out dead.

A Dangerous Pass.-- "About 160 miles from Simla is the Rotang Pass, about 14,000 feet high. It is a very dangerous pass and travellers never cross over it before the 15th of May. The road is closed for seven months in the year on account of snow, and after twelve o'clock in the day a terrible wind blows there which throws travellers over the precipice into a deep valley. Hundreds of people and animals have lost their lives here. A few miles from this place is the source of the river Beas, one of the five great rivers of the Panjab. It is said that the Hindu Saint who compiled the Vedas spent several years in prayer and meditation in a cave near this spot.

"We had many difficulties in crossing this Pass on May 30th. Snow fell and it was very cold, and when we crossed it was snowing. The effect of the bitter wind was painful, for it caused our skin to peel off, but thank God we got over without any loss of life.

Snow slips are bad here. Once a whole village was buried and not a soul was saved. After crossing the Pass we arrived at Khaksar, and preaching in Sissu, Gandhal and in other villages, and arrived in Kyelang, one of the three Moravian mission stations near Tibet.

There are nearly forty Lad'akhi and Tibetan Chris tians in this place, which is about 200 miles beyond Simla, but no European missionary since the War.

We had a good meeting of some thirty people.

In Labors Often.- "I, with my two companions, one of them a Tibetan Christian, now entered Tibet by another route. In Western Tibet we found good opportunities to preach the Gospel and distributed several hundreds of gospel portions and tracts. We visited thirty-seven towns and villages, including Chuprang, Gnanama and Rukhshak. Although some of the lamas were opposed to us the village people heard us gladly. We also visited some monasteries and caves, and the monks and hermits promised to read the Scriptures we gave them, though they did not like us to talk for more than fifteen minutes to them.

In Dangers Often.- "It is not safe and easy to travel in Tibet. There are no roads at all and it is thinly populated country. One may go sixty or seventy miles and never see a village; the only people living in these wildernesses being Gypsies who sleep in tents or caves and live by robbing people. There are also wolves and wild yaks, and many have lost their lives in passing through these desert places. One day I was ahead of my companions when I saw a wild yak come running towards me. Unfortunately there was no tree up which I might climb, but there was a large rock nearby and I ran and climbed up and sat upon it. The furious beast began to run round about the rock, but I was safe, and I began to pray and thank God for this refuge. Thinking about the Rock of Ages I had a wonderful peace in my heart. When my friends saw the yak from a distance they began to shout, and on hearing the noise the Gypsies came out of their tents and caves, and the yak was driven away with stones. We decided to spend the night with the Gypsies; but now there was another danger, for wild people are more dangerous than wild animals. These robbers took everything from us by force, but thank God they did not take our lives. I said to them, 'You have taken away everything from us, but we have something more to give you,' and I began to preach. They listened and were deeply moved, when the Holy Spirit began to work in their hearts. They asked me to forgive them for robbing us, and gave us back everything they had taken from us.

"Now there was another difficulty. The Gypsies prepared tea for us with salt and butter instead of milk and sugar, and when one of them began to pour out for me in a cup, I asked him to let me wash the cup first. In reply he said, 'O how can this be? You are our honored guest, we cannot allow you to cleanse the cup; I will do it for you.' He put out his tongue, which was at least six inches long, and began to lick the inside of the cup. His tongue was long enough to reach the bottom of the cup. When he had finished he filled it with tea, and I then washed the cup and threw the tea away. He was much surprised to see this, and my Tibetan companion explained to him that it was the custom with Indians to wash their hands and vessels before meals. The Gypsy replied that this was a very foolish thing, because in that case the stomach should be washed every day.

"We then drank our tea with sampa or fried barley flour, and after prayer we went to sleep for we were very tired. Next morning, after telling them more about our Savior and praying with them, we continued our journey to a village some thirty miles away."

A World Evangel No, 2.- After his return from Tibet the Sadhu spent the winter of 1921 in evangelistic tours in the Panjab and United Provinces. Several visits also had to be made in preparation for a contemplated visit west again, and also for the assistance and direction of two young sadhus who were receiving training.

Sadhu Sundar Singh's somewhat hurried journey through England, America and Australia in 1920 had the result of taking him West again in 1922.

So, early in the year, Sadhu Sundar Singh reached Bombay to make final arrangements. To his intense joy passports were granted him for Egypt and Palestine as well as for Europe, and an invitation to be the guest in these countries of Sir William Willcocks, K. C. M. G., completed the Sadhu's happiness. Just before sailing he had time to accept an invitation to spend a couple of days with Mahatma Gandhi (a visit of no political significance) in the jungle. On January 28 he embarked on S. S. Caledonia, and leaving the steamer at Port Said, he immediately crossed over to Palestine.

In the Holy Land.- The greatest desire of his heart during sixteen years of Christian life now had its fulfillment, and who can tell what great experiences the Sadhu passed through as he trod in the footprints of the Son of Man! As he passed from place to place every detail of the written records of his Lord poured in upon his mind. The changes of centuries under foreign and cruel domination could not change for him the great fact that it was here his Lord had lived, worked, suffered, died and risen triumphant over death. To him a subtle spiritual atmosphere pervaded every scene, so that his soul overflowed with gladness and the spirit of praise and prayer.

Hours were spent in prayer on Olivet and in the Garden of Gethsemane, during which the Sadhu was conscious of a great reconsecration; it seemed as if Christ Himself stood there, and spoke to him as He had done to His disciples, "Peace be unto you; as my Father hath sent Me, even so send I you," and rising from his knees he knew that he was being sent forth as a witness into all the world.

Through all these wonderful days, passing from Jerusalem through Bethany, Jericho, the Dead Sea, the river Jordan (in which he bathed), Bethlehem, Hebron, Rama, Bethel, Nazareth, Tiberias, Magdala, Capernaum, the Sea of Galilee and other holy spots, the Sadhu was all the time intensely conscious of the personal presence of Christ. "He is always with me wherever I go; He is walking with me at my right hand."

He preached in the Cathedral in Jerusalem and spoke at other services, and then passed on to Cairo, where he preached in the

American Church and again to Coptic Christians in Old Cairo. He visited the Pyramids, and was taken to a church which is supposed to occupy the site of the house where Jesus lived after the flight into Egypt.

The following Sunday the Sadhu preached in Marseilles, and from thence pushed on to Switzerland, to undertake the most strenuous tour of his life.

In Switzerland.- The Sadhu reached Lausanne on February 27, and on the following day commenced his work at a town called Bienne, where a large meeting was held. But in point of numbers this was eclipsed at an open air meeting at Tavannes the next day. People came from all the villages round, over three thousand of them. Many climbed trees to get a better position, and at the close some of them said, "This is a new religion, though it is about the same Savior." The day following snow began to fall, but apparently this in no way hindered the people, who gathered from far and near in a great crowd at a village up amongst the snowy mountains, in order to hear the Old Story told again in a quite new way.

In Geneva Sadhu Sundar Singh preached twice in Reformation Hall where the League of Nations had held its meetings, and although this was a large build ing thousands came and many had to be turned away. He also spoke at a meeting specially for ministers when over two hundred preachers gathered to hear him. From Geneva he passed to Neuchatel, where it was estimated ten thousand came to hear his message and many conversions appear to have taken place. After visiting other towns he then entered German Switzerland, and preached in Basle, Berne, Thun, Zurich, St. Gall and other cities, and on March 29 he completed a heavy program of work in that country.

In Germany.- Passing from Switzerland into Germany the Sadhu wrote: "Yesterday I went to Witten berg, the Cradle of the Reformation. I saw the house in which Martin Luther used to live, and the Church where he used to preach. On the door of the Church he wrote ninety-five articles about the Reformation, and he is buried in the same old Church. This evening I am speaking in the Church." He also spoke to the theological students and professors in that ancient town.

In Halle he met representatives of all the great missionary bodies in Germany at a Conference and spoke to them, and at Leipzig amongst other meetings he preached in the University to the professors and students. At Hamburg, Berlin, Kiel and other cities he preached, and had scarcely time to write even most necessary letters, but he described the meetings as very large and blessed."

In Sweden.- On April 13th he reached Tyringe to commence a month of hard travelling and continuous work, which again covered a large program for cities and villages all over the country. On the way thither he spent a short time at Copenhagen and breakfasted with the Bishop there. After speaking in large meetings in Helsingborg, Lund and other places the Sadhu went to Upsala where he was the guest of the Archbishop, who also translated for him in the Cathedral, University and elsewhere. Just before the arrival of the Sadhu the Archbishop of Upsala had completed writing a book called "Luther and Sundar Singh," a title that called forth some astonishment among the people of the country that the name of Sundar Singh should be coupled with that of one whom all Swedes reverence in a high degree. Some pregnant remarks taken from an article by the Archbishop written for the International Review of Missions on "Christian Mysticism in an Indian Soul" appear in the end of this book.

Passing from the city of Stockholm the Sadhu visited many smaller places. " I am speaking in some of the beautiful villages of this country, and people come in from seventy miles to the meetings." Letters received from those present at those gatherings tell of how special trains had to be run to carry the numbers of people anxious to hear him to the places where he was preaching, and one writer says: "We have never seen such times before." Both in Stockholm and smaller towns the largest buildings could not hold the crowds, and often people arrived some hours beforehand and stood waiting patiently, occasionally in bad weather, until the meetings took place.

Both in Switzerland and Sweden great numbers who had given God no part in their lives, under the Sadhu's ministry surrendered themselves to Christ, and not only was there a revival of spiritual life amongst careless people, but fresh faith was born in the hearts of many as to the power of the Gospel to meet the needs of all nations. This resulted in many giving contributions towards missionary work who had dropped doing so, and others heard the divine call to carry the gospel to souls in other lands where Christ is little known.

The Russian Comtesse de Korff records that "the Sadhu's powerful messages, which we had the privilege to hear, have been translated into Russian and blessed, to many. We pray for him every day, and we shall follow him on our knees everywhere."

In Norway, Denmark and Holland.-- From Sweden the Sadhu went on to Norway, but as the time was getting short he was only able to give ten days to that country. He went to Hurdal, some sixty miles north of the capital and held a large meeting there. In Christiania he had several meetings, one of which was for University students only. Over 3,000 listened breathless^ to his discourse at one of the big gatherings in this city. After visiting other places, on May 24th he left for Denmark.

Even before this time the Sadhu was experiencing great fatigue and much weariness of brain and body, due to continual speaking in a foreign language, with much travelling, and also to the complete strangeness of his surroundings. As in South India in 1918 nobody seemed to realize that he was ever exhausted or needed rest, and the long unbroken toil in an atmosphere as foreign as the languages of the people, wore down his spirit. He longed not only for rest of body but for those periods of quiet meditation and prayer which are the very breath of his existence and source of his power. The need became so insistent that all requests from England had to be cancelled or negated, with the exception of a long promised visit to Keswick. Insistent calls to Finland, Russia, Italy, Greece, Portugal, Servia, Roumania, the West Indies, America and New Zealand had also to be declined, and an immediate return to India following the Keswick Convention was arranged for.

Arrived in Denmark the Sadhu spent three days in Copenhagen, and besides speaking at several meetings he received a call to visit the Dowager Empress of Russia at the King's palace, and on May 27th this remarkable interview took place. At its close when the Sadhu rose to go Her Imperial Majesty desired him to bless her. With humility he replied that he was not worthy to bless anyone, since his hands had once torn up the Scriptures, but that His pierced Hand alone could bless her or anyone.

He then passed on to Liselund, Odense, Aarhus, Herning and Tinglev. At a place called Slagelse the crowds were so great that a meeting had to take place in a large garden, where hundreds of people stood for hours before the commencement. Many occupied the trees and sat on the roofs of surrounding houses, and whilst the Sadhu bore witness to the power of Christ to save men, giving his own experiences in testimony, tears rolled unheeded down the faces of scores of those who heard.

The same thing happened at Nyborg, the Danish Keswick, when deep waves of silent emotion swept over the assembled crowds in token of their response to the personal witness of one who loves his Lord above all else.

On June there was an immense open air meeting at Herning, which vividly recalled to the Sadhu's mind the Syrian Convention in North Travancore at which he had spoken four years before. More than 15,000 people from far and near amidst a great silence received the message of God, which fell on many hearts prepared by His Holy Spirit to receive it. The last meeting in Denmark was at Tinglev, where he spoke to over 9,000 people, and here, as in many other places, numbers bore witness to the spiritual blessing they had received.

On June 5 the Sadhu left for Holland, and, passing through Hamburg, was a second time entertained by Frau Bauer, a lady of the Royal House of Austria and an earnest Christian. In Holland Baron Von Boetzlaer not only entertained him, but also made arrangements for his work. Meetings were held in the pretty old town of De Bilt, in Groningen, Arnheim, Lunderen, Rotterdam, The Hague, and Amsterdam, and at Utrecht the students of four Universities met for a special gathering to hear him.

In Journeys Often.- When the Sadhu landed in England it was apparent to the few old friends who saw him that he was utterly exhausted nervously and physically. Had it been possible for him to leave immediately for India at that time it would have been better for his own sake, but he felt obliged to fulfill a promise to speak at the Keswick Convention, and the time of waiting tried him. Many invitations to stay with friends were declined. One such invitation from a lady who had never seen him, touched the Sadhu's heart. She was a great sufferer herself and found it hard to move abroad, but hearing that he was very tired and suffering from his throat, she not only offered him what would have been the quietest possible place of retirement, but herself undertook a journey of 360 miles to see whether a specialist or any other help was required. The expense of the long journey and the painful fatigue were gladly borne if only she might do something for him.

As week succeeded week it became more apparent that six months in the West of such continuous work had been too great a tax in many ways. The cost of doing this work and of living this life for so long can hardly be realized by those for whom it was done. People who have come under the personal influence of the Sadhu will understand that atmosphere means much to a man who is always working at high pressure in the spiritual realm. For more than sixteen years the Sadhu has been accustomed to a freedom with no bounds of time or place. He loves the open air by night and the open spaces by day, where without any eye to watch he can be alone with his Lord. In such an atmosphere he lives and gathers to himself those reserves of strength and peace which characterize him.

In the rush and hurry of the West no such periods of quiet of even the shortest duration were ever afforded him. Launched into one country after another where dull skies blotted out the sun, and religious work almost took on the aspect of unceasing business; the cast-iron tyranny of arrangements and hours held him like a forest bird imprisoned in an atmosphere that suffocated and sapped his vitality.

In a quiet home in the Isle of Wight he somewhat recovered

his serenity, but even there he could not be prevailed upon to go abroad for exercise. He went away to South Wales for a week-end of preaching, and eventually left for Keswick Convention towards the middle of July.

In England.- "The Sadhu only emerged from his seclusion on two occasions, namely to speak at the Keswick Convention on July 19-22, and to fulfill a long overdue promise to visit Forth in South Wales." A Sunday with three good meetings fulfilled this promise to the Welsh people, and the Sadhu enjoyed his brief ministry among them.

At Keswick he spoke several times. For the benefit of many who could not be present, as well for those who had that privilege his sermon is reproduced further on. At a meeting for ministers the Sadhu spoke on Soul-winning, when he made a significant remark.

"He reminded his hearers that when our Lord called certain of His disciples they were fishermen, and He turned them into fishers of men. But after the crucifixion they went back to their old calling, and when Christ found them again they had ceased to be fishers of men, and were once more fishermen. And some ministers today instead of being fishers of men are merely fishermen,"

Much blessing followed his work. Many consecrated themselves to mission work and hundreds of others received spiritual uplift and inspiration.

From Keswick he went to spend a night with Bishop Welldon at Durham at the Deanery. Writing from here the Sadhu said, "This is not a simple place for a sadhu, but where the Lord sends me there I have to go; sometimes in the palace and often in huts and the open air.

He then went down to London for a few days and on Friday, July 28, he embarked for India on the P. & O. S. S. Plassey, proceeding to Bombay.

To bear witness to the power of Christ as revealed in the gospel and testified to in the heart of the true believer, Sadhu Sundar Singh came West, and thinks his work is done. He felt he owed it to his Lord to bear this witness at all costs, and it has been done.

But in every country and to all people amongst whom this witness has been given the answer also must be given to the question "What owest thou unto thy Lord?" Life cannot go on as it did before he came.

Men must heed or be left worse off than they were before, and of such the Master truly said, "Neither will they be persuaded though one rose from the dead." The supreme need in Europe today is a revival of true religion, and the call of Christ is as insistent now as when he uttered the words, "Take up thy cross and follow Me." In Sundar Singh the transforming power of Christ has had full sway, and obedient to his Lord he follows on, carrying his cross. "Who follows in his train?"

THE SADHU IN LITERATURE

For some years a growing body of literature has been springing up in various forms concerning the Sadhu, both in his own and other countries. Long before his name was known beyond the borders of India, Indians had taken up the task of writing about him. He so far fulfilled the Indian ideal of a Christian holy man that much of what was written in one vernacular was immediately translated into others and was read with avidity all over India.

As he became better known in India, his method of life and work laid him open to criticism, chiefly amongst foreigners ; a criticism not always kindly, and judged by his subsequent history one that showed a lack of perception and understanding of Indian life and ideals. The Sadhu accepted such criticism with the words "If people did not say things against me, I should know there is something seriously wrong."

The marvelous in his life always had its earnest believers, who looked for miracles and took them as fresh and indisputable evidence of his being a man "called of God," whilst others scarcely knew what to think, and thus division of opinion was evoked. The Rev. C. W. Emmett of Ridley Hall, Oxford, discussed in the January number of Hibbert Journal of 1921 what he terms "The Miracles of Sadhu Sundar Singh," dealing chiefly with those mysterious deliverances which have again and again been the Sadhu's experiences in times of great peril. In these events Mr. Emmett sees "a choice between two ways in which God can be thought of as working. Does He help or protect His servants by sending 'an angel' or by the operation of His Spirit on the heart of men? The special inter position of a supernatural agency may at first sight seem attractive to some, but is it not a far grander conception to think of the Spirit of God as working through the personality of such a one as the Sadhu, and so drawing out the response and the latent powers of good in his fellow-men? . . . We do believe that 'there is Some One there.'" The Divine Spirit "passing into holy souls maketh them friends of God and prophets," and working within the limits of that mind of man which is His own creation, is able to thrill and touch them with the immediate consciousness of the presence of "the Beyond that is within."

But with regard to miracles attributed to the Sadhu's own doing Mr. Emmett says nothing. The Sadhu himself says nothing, although he does not trouble to deny their possibility. But frequently he has borne witness to the fact that "there is no power in these hands," and simply claims that the power of Christ in answer to prayer is the only miracle. (See Canon Streeter's book "*The Sadhu*," p. 39.)

Years ago it became clear to the Sadhu that "miracles" detracted from instead of aiding his gospel message. Hence in 1918, when he was making his great tour through the South of India, he took the utmost care to prevent adding fuel to a fire whose burning could serve no true purpose.

His visits to China, Japan and later to the West caused the story of his life, written by different people to be read all over the civilized world. His sermons in English and other languages appeared in booklet form, and magazines in many countries discussed him from all points of view. But through good report and ill the Sadhu calmly passed on his way, the way of God; untroubled, because he feared no man and knew in Whom he had believed.

When he made his first visit West in 1920, many minds of a completely different type from his own were turned to the contemplation and discussion of the man, his experiences, methods of thought and work, and the probable influence of his unique personality and teaching in East and West. As Christianity came out of the East, it is natural that many earnest Christians in western lands should look again to the East, for that new stream of divine life, whose flow should bring a true revival of religion to those myriads upon whom the Great War has cast its black mantle of forget fullness of God.

The Church of the West, blessed with an early vision of the Savior of the world, has yet to mourn its inability to entirely meet the needs of those for whom He died. The simple Gospel, passing through the minds of men throughout the ages, has taken on the color of those minds, and has thus become less potent for its great task; for not in ceremonial appealing to the senses nor yet in mighty organizations is the new birth found. The accretions of the centuries sanctioned by time can offer only a semblance of the life which is in Christ Jesus, and no other life can satisfy. The cry is "Show me a man like Christ." A Swedish Archbishop points to Sundar Singh and says: "The Gospel has not undergone any change in him. . . . In the history of religion Sundar is the first to show the world how the Gospel of Jesus Christ is reflected in unchanged purity in an Indian soul."

To him nothing else matters than the "new creature in Christ Jesus." He has no interest in High Church or Low; Nonconformity in its many forms makes no appeal to him; indeed "it would be heaven on earth," he tells us, if we had not got these things. And as men watch him, study him, write about him, they all agree that through a pure channel men can be and are being stirred to a life that is life indeed.

"Christianity is imperishable," says another writer, "and out of the East it will come again. The Sadhu is perhaps the first of the new apostles to rekindle the fire on dying altars."

A stream of literature in various forms preceded and followed the Sadhu in the countries he visited, and translations flowed into Russia, Italy and other places where he could not go. The Archbishop of Upsala besides writing articles in papers and his book, "Luther and Sundar Singh," contributed an important article to the International Review of Missions, called "Christian Mysticism in an Indian Soul." (April, 1922.) He is a man widely recognized as "an authority on the study of comparative religions," and in the course of his sympathetic article he says:

"What do we learn from this Christian mystic of the land of mystics? A surprising lesson and one that puts to shame all our ingenious speculations as to the higher synthesis between the Bible and India, is the same good news that we know, except that it is The Gospel has not undergone any change in him, but conceived and comprehended with, in certain respects, a surprising interpretation, which can teach us not only something of India but of the

Gospel itself, which heretofore has been monopolized by the Occident, and to some extent transformed in its image. In the history of religion Sundar is the first to show the whole world how the Gospel of Jesus Christ is reflected in unchanged purity in an Indian sold. What is remark able about him is not the fusion of Christianity and Hinduism, but a fresh presentation of genuine Biblical Christianity."

The End
****

Made in the USA
Middletown, DE
31 March 2019